The Two Dreams...

Justin Massé

THE TWO DREAMS

The Two Dreams—Which?

THE TWO DREAMS

BY
JUSTIN MASSÉ

With an Appreciation by PIERRE LOTI
Member of The French Academy

AUTHORIZED TRANSLATION
By FREDERICK ARTHUR

Frontispiece in Color by FRANK J. RIGNEY

NEW YORK
THE DEVIN-ADAIR COMPANY

CONTENTS

PART I

PART II

vii

Contents

To her who taught me sacrifice—my Mother

———

Dreams of to-day! Dreams of yesterday!
Youthful illusions now dead; great hopes which
to-morrow will be dead also! Childish dreams,
grown-up dreams, slain by the garish light of
day, and buried by the hand of time, may this
book cast a gentle glance over your shadowed
memory, like a garland of hope suspended o'er
a tomb.

J. Massé.

LETTRE DE PIERRE LOTI
DE L'ACADÉMIE FRANÇAISE

Monsieur:

J'ai enfin pu parcourir votre manuscrit, je m'en méfiais un peu, je l'avoue, mais j'ai été très-agréablement surpris.

C'est vivant, ému, touchant, cela fait aimer l'enfant qui l'a écrit. Il y a bien quelques petites inexpériences de style dues à la jeunesse, mais de rares qualités d'observation et de sensibilité, etc.

Je vous serre bien cordialement la main.

PIERRE LOTI.

THE TWO DREAMS

PART I

THE TWO DREAMS

CHAPTER I

THE LESSON ON THE VIOLIN

ABEL VERDIER lay dreaming. Alone in his room, surrounded by tins and boxes of groceries of all shapes and sizes, he lay back in his chair, his violin pressed to his breast, waiting for his lesson to begin. As he tilted the chair backward and forward, he swung gently to and fro as if in accompaniment to his dream.

Of what was he thinking, this boy of scarcely fourteen, with his serious air, and his long locks of golden hair which curled over his slightly wrinkled forehead?

Of what was he thinking? Of the ap-

3

proaching holidays, perchance, with their long and beautiful hours full of joy and of sunshine?

Scarcely; for he left school a month ago, and to-morrow he was to become a townsman and enter upon his apprenticeship.

Perchance, then, it was the approaching farewell which filled his thoughts?

Again no, for the bright light in his eyes told that the dream was a happy one. Aye, it was beautiful, as for the thousandth time it passed before his eyes, fascinating them, blinding them almost with the bright flame of a desire burning ever more and more brightly.

It had come to him one day, four years ago and more, long after the death of his father, whom he could scarcely remember. His widowed mother, owner of a small general dealer's shop in the village, was left defenceless in a neighbourhood where customers are hard and exacting, and where

4

egoism, jealousy and hatred towards the weak and suffering have taken the place of the gentle pity and tender charity of other days.

One night, when he found his mother in tears, and realized more vividly than ever before what she had suffered and what she was destined to suffer in the future, he shut himself up in his room and wept. Then, taking his violin from its case, he began to play, and as he played the instrument whispered consolation and many a soothing message, until joy took the place of sorrow, and his tears ceased to flow. His love and his sympathy and pity for her who was all the world to him, and perhaps some glimpse too of his new-born talent, suggested to his mind a wondrous thought, and gave birth to a desire in his heart and a ray of hope in his soul, which spoke in mysterious language like a murmured caress.

"Work, work," it said, "and one day thou

too shalt be an artist like thy father's friend."

Artist! The magic of the word dazzled him, troubled him almost with its delicious charm, as he hugged closer still his beloved violin, which sounded tremulously in his grasp.

.   .   .   .   .   .

For the first time Passion made herself known to him, and Genius stood almost at the door.

Artist! How he had dreamt of it! How he had seen himself already celebrated, and his mother peaceful and happy at his side! He swore that she should weep no more, that the world should no longer have power to make her suffer, that she should no longer need to work!

That day, as he locked his instrument in its long black case, he resolved to become an artist.

6

From that time onward he had never ceased to cherish this idea, beautifying it with all the force of his childish imagination. It was constantly before his mind, and he was dreaming of it now as he waited for his last violin lesson before starting for the town to commence his apprenticeship. For it was necessary for him to learn some trade whereby to earn his daily bread and to pay for the violin lessons until he should be ready to enter the Conservatoire.

He had decided to learn hair-dressing; not that he had any taste in that direction, but because it was a fairly easy trade, not difficult to learn, and one whereat he could begin at once to earn some money.

Suddenly the sharp ring of a bell startled Abel out of his reverie. He rose and looked out. It was not his professor, but a customer. He returned to his chair disappointed. The expression of his face denoted anxiety and impatience. On this, the

7

last occasion on which he should meet the professor, he had resolved to put to him a question which hitherto he had not dared to ask.

He had no doubt of himself, yet he longed for some one else—some one who had deciphered the secret of his soul—to say: "Fear not: thy dream is not beyond thy reach."

Abel was dreaming again, when suddenly, moved by some impulse within him, by some powerful and imperious artistic passion not strange to him, he rose pale and trembling, picked up his violin, and possessed by a sudden nervous inspiration, he began to play.

Then something shuddered in the wood and came to life; then something chanted and wept beneath the trembling fingers, beneath the bow now smoothly sliding, anon bounding over the strings as if intoxicated with sound. Then something sweet and

8

melancholy—not a chord, for chords feel not—but rather Abel's very soul itself, entering into the instrument, animated it with its breath, causing it for the time to live as part of his life.

A second time the bell rang, but Abel heard it not, for his soul had passed whole and entire within the instrument.

M. Nirg, the old professor, advanced silently to the threshold of the half-opened door, and stood listening, surprised and overcome as he watched his young pupil. Never before had he heard the like. The melody not only pleased his ear: it penetrated his soul with a new and unknown charm, filling his heart with a strange and indefinable emotion.

It was no piece of music, artistically composed and learned by heart, no complicated song with carefully studied harmonies, but rather an improvisation, a spontaneous fountain of sound drawn out by the passion, or maybe by the genius, of the player, just as instinct creates song in the bird. A long and wondrous melody, almost sublime, it issued from a soul troubled by desire and filled with enthusiasm by its hope.

Now the melody languished; the discords grew softer and then vanished; the notes seemed to blend into one another, as if the player's soul, worn out by the effort, were slowly detaching itself from the instrument; then a final melancholy note faded and died away, like a sigh epitomizing all that had preceded it.

Abel, his nerves relaxed as if fatigued by the sustained effort, let his violin slip from his hands on to the table.

"Good day, my young friend. I congratulate you. You play with your whole soul."

The boy started violently, as, with a heightened colour, he wrung the professor's hand, murmuring an apology.

M. Nirg gazed interrogatively into the eyes of his pupil, who felt uncomfortable and embarrassed.

"What have you been playing? What is the name of that piece?"

"It has no name; I was playing I know not what, while I was waiting for you—just to pass the time," explained the boy, somewhat abashed.

The old professor did not pursue the subject, merely smiling in reply, and the lesson began.

When the prescribed exercise had been repeated several times, M. Nirg, after giving his pupil a few practical hints and telling him to play over constantly certain difficult studies with a view to gaining an increased power of technique, placed on the music-stand a composition he had brought with him.

"Listen," he said. "This is a Meditation. You will play it after me." And the professor, who knew the Meditation by heart, summoned all his art to interpret it.

As the last note died softly away, and the bow, moving gently, gently, over the strings, ceased at last almost imperceptibly, Abel very diffidently took up his instrument. His hand trembled as he did so.

"It is your turn now. One—two—three —*piano* to begin with," said the professor as he counted the first few bars.

At first the notes sounded forced and feverish. Abel did not feel at ease; he was troubled by the thought of the professor standing there, close by, listening to him. But soon he forgot the other's presence; and, as he forgot, he began to play to himself alone. Then, as he penetrated to the inner meaning of the music, his interpretation changed; the intonation grew clearer; fresh harmonies more full of life and enchantment filled the air, mingling and interlacing one with the other, until they blent together in one harmonious whole.

M. Nirg, as he listened intently, found himself completely under the spell of that magic of sound which troubled and yet enchanted all that was most tender in his soul, echoing in his artist nature like some impalpable and mysterious chant.

Any one entering the room might have wondered whether the real professor was indeed the old man who stood listening with such astonishment and admiration. For the professor had never heard his pupil play like this before. He knew the boy was gifted for his age, and yet he had hesitated to believe him to be a real artist. He had never sounded the depth of the boy's shy nature, nor would he have done so now had he not surprised his pupil when the player thought he was alone.

When he had entered the room, he had

unexpectedly come upon Abel at the moment when he was, as it were, "letting himself go," and he was thus able to surprise that growing shy genius which had never before dared to disclose itself.

When the boy finished playing, he looked towards his master questioningly; but, at the sight of a tear upon those rugged features, he dropped his eyes and said nothing.

"That is very good. I am pleased with you. Go on working regularly and you will arrive at the goal," said the old man.

They talked of Abel's departure; of the trade he was going to learn; of the new music-master who would teach him in his new home.

Whether from shyness or from forgetfulness, Abel never asked in that last interview the question which he so longed to have answered. But words are not always necessary! A look, a gesture, a tear, may suffice.

M. Nirg left his pupil after a short but

touching farewell. He had, he said, two more lessons to give before he returned home to Milly, which lies five kilometres from Vally.

Standing at the window, Abel watched the professor depart, and saw him stop to talk to Mme. Verdier, who appeared to be listening with profound attention.

What was the professor saying? Surely they must be talking of him.

Not long after, when his mother entered the room and embraced him, Abel understood, and his soul was filled with an abundant joy.

CHAPTER II

ADIEU TO THE WOODS

HALF an hour later, Abel was walking down a path which traverses a small wood and leads to the river.

All round him stretched the valley, with its fields of wheat and oats, its meadows and its vineyards; that valley whose every path he knew, whose woods and thickets he had so often explored, whose streams, flowers and murmurs were all so familiar; that valley in whose green cradle his boyish years had been passed, and where he had dreamed and lulled his childhood to repose, where he had picked his first flowers and seen his earliest visions; that valley which had never been absent from his sight, and which he was fated to leave on the morrow for the first time. And now he gazed on it all, on the harvest fields, the clumps of trees, the patches of green grass with their pale flowers, with the eyes of one who looks on things that he may never see again.

He walked on between two fields of corn, full of life, which rustled on each side of him. The ears, moved by the wind, bent as he passed them, emitting an odour of meal and warm straw which mounted to his head and recalled the day long ago, when he, a very small boy, had wandered in among the corn, hiding his little yellow head behind the golden ears to frighten his grandmother and his father, who were following quietly at some distance.

How many years had passed since then, since those times of his childhood! And yet the face of nature had not changed. The same harvests waved and quivered in the lightest breeze; the same flowers, red poppies and blue corn cockles, seemed to play at hide and seek behind the corn stalks, watching him furtively, timidly, these with their large blood-red eyes, and those with their little pale blue ones, as if they feared to be seen.

Abel entered a grove he had often visited. At the sound of his footsteps the birds ceased their song amid the branches, but soon, recognizing their young friend, they resumed their twittering with more energy than before.

The river Yonne was near at hand, and Abel could see the water through the trees. Whiffs of fresh fragrance from the stream were wafted towards him.

He sat down on the grass near the bank, which the water lapped with a slight sound scarcely perceptible, and watched the thousand little glittering wavelets as the breeze played upon them. How happy he was here! How good it was once more to rest amid this kindly nature, by the side of this murmuring water, in this wood so full of friendly voices!

Little birds, here for a season only, singing among the trees, sing your best for your departing friend, for he can never hear you again, nor will you ever see him more!

Abel pondered, his eyes still fixed on the water, and thought succeeded thought, pressing one upon the other in his brain as rapidly as the light waves he was watching rose, danced, pressed upon one another and crushed one another as they flowed past.

Where would he be to-morrow?

In the town, no doubt; but the town was to him the unknown, the unknown which at one and the same time attracted and frightened him, the unknown which he would give so much to fathom. He seemed to be asking an answer from the waves as they passed by, running down stream in little bounds.

"O you who come from so far away, little wanderers that you are, perchance you have passed by the walls of the town where I shall be to-morrow! Tell me, in your language which I can understand, what it is like, and whether the houses and fields and the woods which surround them resemble those that I love! Tell me, shall I be happy there?"

Ah! if only some of those fields in the valley had belonged to him, those fields he had so often coveted, he would never have left them, as so many others had done, in order to seek the town!

But he owned nothing here: the land with its abundant harvests grew nothing for him, nothing but the wild flowers and plants which he loved to pick among the grass by the side of the footpaths.

Besides, he must needs quit the country, for away there beyond the town lay his future, and the happiness of which he had dreamed for himself and for those he loved.

Slowly the sun sank towards the horizon. Now it was behind the little covert, some of its rays piercing between the branches and the leaves and gilding Abel's blond hair as they rested on it.

"I shall always see the sun, anyhow," said the boy as he felt the sunbeams' caress, and he turned towards the light, and let the rays, which the sun shot through a thousand small obstacles, fall on him and dazzle him.

He looked at his watch, and rose hurriedly. It was five o'clock, and his mother had told him to fetch his small brother from school. He hurried away without turning his head, as if he feared lest, by looking and thinking and remembering, he might be overcome by his regrets and might be unable to tear himself away from this little corner of his native land which he had loved so deeply ever since his childhood.

When, however, he was a long way off, and about to take the route which twists sharply to the left towards the village, he turned to the river and the wood, taking in the whole valley in one long, loving look; then, half closing his eyes, in which the tears lay hidden, he raised his fingers to his lips and stretched them out towards the valley in one farewell kiss.

At this moment there arose a trembling all through the valley, as a breeze, strong and yet very gentle, passed over it like a sigh, touching Abel's lips ere it died away. It was his beloved Nature saying adieu to him—Nature returning his farewell kiss.

He turned sadly away.

Before going home, he called at the school for his little brother Joel, who sprang into his arms, showing him a small square of green paper, a good mark which the child's master had given him because his sum in addition had been well done. Little

Joel beamed on his brother as he received the latter's congratulations, when suddenly a shadow passed across the child's blue eyes and troubled them.

"Is it true that you are going away to-morrow—eh, big brother?"

The tender anxiety of the questioning voice would have struck Abel even if it had not been visible in the child's face.

"Yes, it is true, little Joel; thou knowest it."

"And why are you going?"

Abel smiled without answering.

"Tell me, why are you going?" persisted the child.

"You know I am going to learn a trade and to work."

This answer made the child pensive.

"But when will you come back?"

"I shall come back, I shall come back . . . I don't exactly know when," said Abel, hesitatingly; but seeing the child's sadness and trouble, and the tears welling up in the tender little eyes, he added at once:

"I shall surely come back soon."

"And when you come back, will that be for always?"

The boy looked at his small brother in surprise. How grown up the child was! How closely he questioned Abel on things which stirred the heart.

"Tell me, big brother, afterwards shall you stay with us always?"

"Yes; later on I shall return and never leave you more. But before that, I must work, and thou also. Thou must go on working steadily."

There was silence for a space, while Abel thought of the day when his dream should be realized, and he should call those whom he loved to be with him always, and should make them happy.

"Yes, little brother, one day we won't

leave one another any more; but if that is to be, you must learn to be very good."

The child's eyes grew bright again and deliciously blue, like a clear sky in spring.

When they reached their home, "the grocer's shop at the corner," as it was called, they passed the wide front with its decoration of samples displayed to catch the eye, and continued on their way without pausing.

There were at that moment many customers in the shop, as always happened when evening came, much to the envy of the other grocers, whose customers were comparatively few. Mme. Verdier attracted this numerous clientèle through her good-natured complaisance and her perfect honesty.

She was, in the language of the countryside, "Very obliging and very easy to deal with."

Abel and his little brother turned down the alley which led to their back yard. When they entered the house their grandmother was peeling potatoes for the evening meal. She greeted them with an old woman's sweet smile, calm, happy and unaffected, such as one sees only on the faces of children and the aged.

"Good evening, grandmother."

Joel soon found his way into his grandmother's arms, while Abel, smiling, entered the shop and began to help his mother to serve the customers.

CHAPTER III

DEPARTURE

VERY late that night, when the shop was closed and little Joel in bed, the packing of Abel's luggage took place.

He stood, pensive and a little sad, watching his mother and his grandmother as they carefully laid at the bottom of a long black trunk his linen, his other garments, his dressing things, and all those numberless articles whose disappearance increases the void we leave behind us.

The box was soon filled, but it still remained open, although nothing was lacking to complete it, not even a tear which dropped from his mother's eyes and lost itself among the pile of white linen.

27

While Mme. Verdier, after closing the lid, began to cord the box with her son's assistance, the old grandmother gazed sadly at the great empty cupboard, now stripped of all that had belonged to her grandson, bereft of those garments which she herself had made for him, void of the linen she had so often washed and ironed, void of everything that could remind her of him.

.   .   .   .   .   .

The next morning, very early, the coach, which usually passed noisily, shaking the window panes as it rolled along, came to a sharp halt in front of the grocery shop. At the same moment the small white door opened and Mme. Verdier and her son came out, followed by the grandmother and little Joel. The latter was crying piteously.

Abel began to say good-bye. Two small nervous arms, which would not let go, clung round his neck, and he was obliged at last to unclasp them. Then he turned to embrace his grandmother, who stood pale and trembling, her weary and sunken eyes still holding enough tears to weep for the departure of the grandson whom perhaps she should never see again.

As he pressed her aged and fragile form to his heart, touching with his lips her pale, thin cheek, cold with the chill of age, he realized that perhaps he held his grandmother in his arms for the last time, and feeling the tears welling up in his eyes, he hurried into the coach and sat down by his mother as the heavy vehicle rumbled away.

Abel leaned out of the window to catch the last signals of farewell, and to see once more his poor old granddame smiling at him through her tears. Then he remembered the dream of happiness which he secretly bore along with him, and thought with sorrow that perhaps she would never know of its existence.

When the two small figures disappeared,

and he could no longer distinguish anything, he turned his eyes away and began
gazing round him over the plain. The valley he had so long known and would see
no more except in thought, seemed to slide
past him as he gazed—that dear valley
where such abundant and shimmering harvests lay stretched out in graceful majesty.
He had seen the fields successively grow
green and then golden under the thousand
burning kisses of the sun. Soon they would
fall in shining copper beneath the sharp
and whistling sickles, and this year he
would not be there to see them die.

His eye passed in a rapid farewell over
the paths he had so often trod, the stream
by whose banks he had passed so many
happy hours, and whose murmurings he
seemed still to hear within his heart.

Farther back he saw the woods into which
he had so often plunged, listening to the
sighing of the wind and the twittering of

the birds as their voices blent and mingled in a long and sweet harmony, wafted through the leaves and the branches which waved gently, as if in response to the sound.

There in those woods had he received his first and his best music lessons; those lessons which Nature gives us in these exquisite and enchanted solitudes, and it was there that his soul, captivated and enthralled, had become as it were impregnated with dreamy harmonies.

All that could be seen of the village was a confused mass of houses piled together at the end of the valley. It had almost vanished now, and trees, bushes, and fields—nay, the valley itself—seemed following it and disappearing also.

Abel felt as if everything he had loved, everything which had captivated him in this little corner of the world, and had found its way gently into his heart, were now suddenly going.

It seemed to him that the very soul of nature, which had in some way mingled with his own child-soul, consoling him in his sorrows and lulling him in his reveries, was now detaching itself from it.

"Thou art sad; of what thinkest thou?"

Abel, recalled to the present, drew himself up, somewhat ashamed at having given way to sadness, and smiled brightly at his mother, as if to show that he was brave and almost glad to be leaving home.

And why, indeed, should he be sad? Was not everything happening just as he had wished, and was not this departure the very thing he had longed for? Had he not waited impatiently for this day, when, full of youth and hope, he could satisfy his great ambition?

And then why such regret at leaving a place where nature and inanimate objects were good and kind, but where men were so indifferent, so selfish and at times so hard;

a place where, although he left behind him such precious souvenirs and a home with so much love, he had nevertheless learned what hatred is, had seen those he loved suffer, and where his mother had so often been made to weep?

Yes, he ought rather to rejoice that he was going away. A new life was beginning for him, and in proportion as he separated from the old one, would he feel his coming manhood. New forces, unknown aspirations, like a flowing sap spreading through his whole being, caused his heart to burn within him, and he who yesterday had feared lest his dream were too great, now found to his delight that he possessed a new source of ardour and enthusiasm to carry forward so great a hope.

The coach came to a stop in front of a tall white house. It was the railway station. From within came the sharp, persistent sound of a bell, whose voice, like a far-away and mysterious call from the unknown, brought trouble to Abel's soul.

A few minutes later, and the train bore the travellers far and ever farther from their village home.

Abel sat with his head half bent towards the window, watching the tall telegraph poles, the trees, the bushes, which flew past at a prodigious pace, while farther away the country-side, borne past in a slower and more stately progress, spread out its vast plains and varied contours in endless variety, the green summits of the hills standing out in graceful contrast against the azure sky.

Intoxicated by a sort of vertigo, the boy felt a strange, wild joy as he was carried amid this flight of all visible things farther and farther towards the future, nearer and nearer towards the glory and happiness of which he had dreamed.

.   .   .   .   .   .

It was about one o'clock in the afternoon when Mme. Verdier and her son entered the hair-dressing saloon of M. Moreau. They had just seen his name in glittering gold letters upon a white door-plate.

Dazzled by the mirrors and the reflections they made, and almost suffocated by the vague scent of numberless perfumes, Mme. Verdier advanced towards the two assistants, each of whom held in his hand a newspaper which he had been reading.

They rose, bowing.

The elder, who seemed about twenty-five years of age, had a hard and expressive face, and looked at her out of cold, blasé eyes which seemed to freeze one as one encountered them. The other, about seventeen, had a ruddy complexion not yet bleached by cosmetics, and his thick, coarse, black hair was divided by a faultless parting. They both wore the customary yellow jacket.

"I beg your pardon—I wish to see M. Moreau."

"What name shall I say?"

"Abel Verdier and his mother."

The younger assistant vanished immediately down a passage, while the other silently took from a drawer an elegant little clipping-machine which he inspected minutely, turning it over and over between his long, pointed fingers.

Abel looked round him. The walls were adorned with graceful pictures and long mirrors; in front of him, on a marble toilet table, stood a row of shining scent-bottles which were reflected in the glass behind them so that they appeared double. There was an air of tawdriness about the place.

Here, then, he was destined to live for two years, surrounded by these mirrors; in this perpetual glitter, which already fatigued his eyes; in this factitious atmosphere saturated with perfume; with this cold and

36

contemptuous assistant. The thought gave him pain.

At this moment M. Moreau appeared. He was a small man, fairly young, with a long black beard which half concealed a small and meagre face whence two black eyes looked out at you, vivacious, sparkling, and never still.

He conducted his visitors into the dining-room.

"Ouf! If he wants an apprentice, the monkey, it's about time," said the younger assistant, with a sigh.

"Lucky dog! You'll live the life of an independent gentleman now."

"Certainly I'm not going to refuse a chance; I give way willingly to the young comrade."

"Poor little devil! I am sorry for him if he doesn't like scrubbing," replied the other in mock pity.

"Bah! He'll like it! *L'appetit vient en*

mangeant! I wish him a happy time of it. Bah! when I think that I, too, had to do that job once!"

"Don't abuse it. It has its good side. I'm almost sorry I've done with it!" And the young fellow, having delivered himself of this remark, burst into a peal of laughter, while the other—M. André, as he was called in the house—contented himself with a smile. He was in a good temper that evening, a rare occurrence with him.

Meanwhile, in the dining-room they discussed Abel and the trade he was to learn. Mme. Verdier spoke of his love for the violin, and of his ability, and asked that he might have at least an hour a day for studying and two hours a week for his lessons.

It was arranged that the agreement should not be signed then and there, but in some months' time, so that Abel could say whether he liked the work.

Then Mme. Verdier asked to see the apprentice's bedroom. M. Moreau led her to it, while Abel and the younger assistant carried up the luggage.

At last they arrived before a door.

"It's in there," said the hairdresser in his weak voice, as he showed Abel's mother into a sort of alcove with low walls and a very narrow window, which scarcely admitted any light, and which M. Moreau hurriedly opened, more for the sake of fresh air than to lessen the obscurity of the garret.

When she saw the dark, low-roofed attic, with its dusty walls, which was to do duty as a bedroom for her boy, Mme. Verdier's heart sank, but she didn't like to say anything.

Poor mother, who wished to do better for your son, you little thought that the poor apprentice must be content with a dark garret squeezed in under the roof, in order that

39

the customers may be received in splendid
saloons, and the employers lodged in spa-
cious, well-furnished chambers!

Poor woman! Many who come from the
country are like you. When they pass
through the streets of the town, admiring
its handsome shop fronts and façades, and
watching themselves reflected in dazzling
mirrors, they look with envy at the wide
windows and muslin curtains, but they
don't see up there, above the mirrors, above
the fine white hangings, above everything
which pleases the eye, that little window
hidden among the roofs, which is the only
opening to a wretched garret whose darkness is never illumined by a single ray of
sunshine, but where human beings, sons of
the soil, maybe, who once dwelt in light
and liberty, live stifled and enclosed.

.   .   .   .   .   .

On the platform at the railway station,
lost among a crowd of passengers coming

and going, a woman about forty years of age, small and simply dressed, was talking to a young lad who was leaning slightly towards her and looking from time to time at the great station clock whose hand stood at the half hour. It was Mme. Verdier, who had only a quarter of an hour longer to spend with Abel, and to say all that she had to say. She gave her last instructions hurriedly.

"Above all, write to me constantly, and don't do imprudent things, or go out too often at night!"

"All right, Mother," he replied, with a slight inclination of the head.

She went on.

"I am afraid you may grow weary and discouraged"—her voice had the sound of suppressed tears. Abel, too, could scarce contain himself, and he longed at that last moment to make her a partaker of his hopes. A wild desire to tell her everything took possession of him; he wanted to reveal the secret of his childhood, kept hitherto locked up in the recesses of his heart, but not daring, and fearing that to do so might be premature, he merely answered, with many hints in his voice and words:

"Don't worry; I am no longer a child. I shall be strong, and you will be satisfied with my work."

All at once, he saw the tears running down his mother's cheeks, and he thought to himself:

"Weep not, little Mother; I know you must leave me and return home alone to resume your hard task and to continue to suffer, but you don't know how I mean to work to bring near the day when I shall make you happy!"

A loud noise made itself heard. It was the train.

Fearing that she might not have time, his mother dropped her parcels on the ground and took her son in her arms, holding him there for some seconds.

As their two hearts came in contact, pressed together in one final embrace, the tears were about to flow when a loud whistle and the noise of the engine held them back. Elbowed, dragged along by the passengers hurrying to secure places, Mme. Verdier was at last separated from her son.

After a few moments' halt, the iron monster gave a whistle, struggled violently, and then resumed its course through space, slowly at first, then faster, regardless of those carried off or of those left behind, knowing neither whom it was separating nor whom uniting.

Among the many faces peering out of the windows of the departing train, there was one very pale and sad, with lips tightly pressed together to keep back the tears so as to smile back for the last time. It was Mme. Verdier.

As long as it was visible, she continued to keep her eyes on Abel's little grey coat. Then, when everything grew dim, she closed her eyes, to keep before them as long as possible the image of her son.

When she opened them she saw the huge, confused mass of the town already in the distance, as it raised aloft its thousands of roofs and chimneys, and towering above them all, the superb Gothic cathedral silhouetting the delicate and harmonious lines of its lace-like masonry against the azure sky.

There, in the city, in the great noisy, feverish, agitated throng which filled her with fear as its evil breath rose upwards in a dark pall of smoke, she had left her son alone.

·   ·   ·   ·   ·   ·

Abel was indeed alone. When he returned to his room he leaned out of his little

44

window, and there, in the heart of the great city as yet unknown to him, he began to dream.

He began to dream, and what he saw with his fixed glance lost among the roofs, was the train which was carrying past plains, hills and woods her whom he loved more than all else, and who had just parted from him—his mother.

How far away she must be now!

His imagination pictured an enormous and ever growing distance between himself and his mother, and the thought filled him with fear in spite of himself.

Yes; she who had always been close to him, how far away she must be now!

Henceforth it must be so. She could not be what she had hitherto been in his life. He would only see her occasionally until the day arrived when—but ought he even to think of that? And would that day, seen in his dreams, ever really come?

Alas! How solitary he was, and how he realized his loneliness.

Poor Abel! Where was his enthusiasm now? Where was the hope that had sustained him that very morning? While his mother had been with him he had not thought how hard it would be to leave her. He had even longed to be free so as to realize that secret which he had never confided to any one. But now that she had gone, now that he was indeed alone, he experienced a strange and painful sensation of solitude and emptiness.

Poor boy! When you dreamed as you wandered along the footpaths of your country-side, you saw the future through the eyes of that dazzling and gentle nature which encompassed you, and which gently fostered thought. At a distance, all seemed so simple and ready to bend to your desires as easily as the reeds and grasses round you bent before the passing breeze.

46

You did not foresee the suffering and the tears, or rather you carefully kept them out of your dream, and now at its commencement they come down upon you, casting a shadow—the shadow of reality—across the dazzling brightness of your vision.

Abel, weary of thinking, closed the window, and was on the point of throwing himself on his bed to weep in despair, when his eye caught a long, dark object half hidden in the shadows.

It was his violin!

He was wrong just now: he was not alone, for this friend still remained to console him for the past and to inspire him with hope for the future.

He took it from its case, pressed it lovingly to him, seizing the neck with trembling fingers, and directly his flesh came in contact with the wood, and his soul in touch with the instrument, sounds issued forth,

47

blending in a sweet and plaintive melody, revealing the wounds of a suffering soul and the regrets, the sighs, and the tears caused by sorrow.

It was the cry of a soul in mourning, the melancholy chant of farewell wafted by a child of the country, a widow's son, in the midst of a great city, towards the land of the dear ones he had left.

When Abel ceased playing peace had re-entered his heart, and he began again to hope.

His violin, his only remaining friend, had consoled and fortified him. Now he felt himself strong.

He left his room, and descending the stairs, began his new apprenticeship.

CHAPTER IV

THE NEW LIFE

THE first few days seemed long to Abel, suffering as he did from homesickness and a sort of vague longing for the past.

The new life, too, enclosed and restricted as it was, was particularly galling to one accustomed to a free, open-air life under the broad blue sky. The greater part of his time was passed in perpetual polishing of floors, woodwork and marble furniture. He might have been seen mounted on a stool, dusting a mirror, or behind a pile of folded napkins which he rolled up one by one and put into rings. His body was there, but his soul and his spirit were far away at home, in the place to which his thoughts were constantly returning in spite of himself.

For the first few evenings Abel accompanied the others to the cabaret in search of distraction, but there he found that while the others could amuse themselves, he was more bored than ever.

Everything there disgusted him: the dim light over the tables, thrown by the rows of gas-jets which succeeded one another until they disappeared down dark passages; the coarse pleasures of the drinkers leaning heavily over the tables; the ring of laughter which sounded false; the equivocal or obscene remarks which spread a grin over the faces of the hearers or lit their eyes with unholy flames.

One evening he refused to go to the cabaret any more, and the two assistants laughed at him.

He didn't care for these two assistants.

They had a knack of laughing at everything, even at the most serious things. Nothing seemed to surprise them; they seemed to have tasted and to have become surfeited with everything.

Abel never felt at ease with them; he had neither their temperament, their thoughts, their desires, nor their words, and above all, he had not their laughter. So he shut himself up as far as possible, fearing to reveal his true self.

One afternoon, however, when he was playing the violin up in his room with all his usual passion, the door which he had forgotten to lock opened gently, and a head appeared, and then another, both faces lit by the same indefinable smile.

Abel noticed nothing, for he was completely absorbed. He was playing the piece which had once drawn a tear from his late master's eyes.

All at once a mocking sound was heard,

and the boy nearly dropped the violin as he started and stopped playing.

Abel had been caught unawares, and against his wish he had revealed a glimpse of his talent and laid bare a corner of his soul before these two mocking young fellows. ，.

An almost savage expression of displeasure showed on his features as they approached.

"You're a nailer," said the younger. "One can see that you are studying. Begin again, so that we may listen."

"Yes, play that over again," said M. André, backing up his companion in a blasé tone which increased Abel's irritation.

"It wouldn't interest you," said Abel, determined not to play again while they were there. They might laugh at him in any other way as much as they liked, but not in connection with his beloved fiddle.

"Wouldn't interest us? What do you

take us for? We aren't philistines; we understand music."

"I should rather imagine so!" exclaimed the other contemptuously. "The gentleman expects to be pressed, I see. Now then, youngster, no affectations! I'll beat the time—one, two, three, eh?"

"I tell you it wouldn't interest you, so it's useless to insist."

"Play something else, then—a valse or a romance. *'J'ai tant pleuré,'* for instance, or a polka."

"I don't know any."

"Here's a fine fiddler who can't play *'Viens poupoule'!* Hand me the fiddle, then: I'll play!"

Abel's only answer was to replace his instrument in the case, closing the lid with a sharp click. He was growing weary.

"Steady there—steady, you young knave!" cried the younger assistant.

Then they left the room, M. André exclaiming in his most sarcastic tone: "One would think his violin was made of sugar!"

Similar scenes often tormented Abel and didn't incline him to love his new life. They made him conscious of certain brutal realities which perforce tended to modify the dream in which he took such pleasure.

Two months passed, and Abel began to accustom himself to his new life. He thought less of the past and the present, and more of the future, which latter continued to smile on him.

But the moments of hope and enthusiasm when his joy seemed to overflow, were always succeeded by periods of lassitude and discouragement. Then the days and hours seemed of interminable length, and his two years of apprenticeship a time which would never end. Then doubts came. He saw his dream as something far away which would never come to pass, but which would one day vanish, and then he would be compelled to pass all his life in an obscure existence which he loathed.

At such moments he fell a victim to weariness; he felt a vague disgust at having to recommence the same duties day after day, to resume each morning the tasks of the previous night; to listen again and again to the same conversations.

He was suffering from the void which he felt both around and also within him. He was like some poor young plant torn from its native soil and replanted in another one, hard and cold, where it was deprived of light and heat. What he needed was a little of the light which comes not from this world, and which gives warmth and comforts the soul.

What Abel lacked above all else was that faith which sustains the young heart at fifteen, when love and hope are a necessity, that faith which gives so great an import to our humblest actions, and teaches us to love our daily life, with its ever recurring tasks, its sighs and its tears, by revealing to us another.

His mother was a Christian, and at her knees, his eyes fixed upon hers, he had felt as a child something unspeakably sweet enter into his heart as he learned to believe and to pray. Later he had made his first communion, but alas! after that . . .

After that came the world, with its examples, its talk, its jeers, its indifference, and all that was most delicate and impressionable in his soul had grown hardened.

Now he believed no longer. He had felt the divine flame grow less and less, and ere it died another had already taken its place, one that he had cherished with love and nourished with chimeras—the flame of human glory. And this flame did not *warm* his heart; it burned and consumed it.

CHAPTER V

GOD RETURNS

ABEL had just finished his violin lesson, and as he stood in his lonely room, thinking over the congratulations which he had just received from his master, M. Choutot, he was happy and gave free rein to his thoughts.

He saw himself three years ahead, a student at the Conservatoire. His masters were proud of him, and he made his mark, obtaining the first violin scholarship.

Other and sweeter dreams followed in succession, and his heart beat as if the joys he dreamed of were already realized.

He dreamed no more. He lived. No longer was he the young apprentice resting awhile from his labours, nor yet the pupil just released from his lesson, but the young artist, celebrated and admired, which he had promised himself he would become.

His mother, too, was no longer a poor dealer, obliged to conform to all the demands and caprices of her customers, but a mother surrounded by homage and respect, and as welcome as her son in the salons of the metropolis.

Poor lad! this was the guise in which he foresaw the future.

All at once, in the midst of all these intoxicating thoughts, of all these evocative images which fascinated and subdued his mind, a question, terrible and full of anguish, presented itself.

When all this happened, would his mother be still alive? And even if she lived to pass many happy years by his side, a day would come when he must part from her for ever, a day when death would take her

58

from him—nay, a day when he himself must die and nothing would remain of either except a little ashes within a tomb. He saw that tomb, there before his eyes, and for the first time in his life the spectre of Death laid an icy hand upon his soul.

Death to him, who no longer believed, meant nothingness, in which all he had ever loved, hoped, possessed, would be lost for ever, and in which he, too, one day would be lost as they were.

This thought of nothingness made him afraid. Something within him, desiring to live, rebelled, revolted, raged, trembled at this terrible destiny of death. To cease to exist for all eternity, to keep nothing whatever of life, not even a remembrance; to receive nothing more from it—not even a vague thought enveloped in a dream! No, it could not be; the thought hurt him. That which he felt so strongly alive within him, that which moved within him when, mastered by his inspiration, he began to play, could never be annihilated. No; his soul, with all its desires and hopes, might quit his body, as it seemed to quit his violin when he ceased playing, but only for a time. Otherwise it would be too terrible—where would be the use of life? Where was the use of all his struggles if death was to finish all? No; death did not do that. He would believe as he had in childhood; he felt the need of God, and suddenly his whole being, filled with an immense desire, turned to Him.

Yes, he wished to believe; he *did* believe; his soul was illumined by a new joy; the abyss which had terrified him was filled, and it was God who filled it.

It was God whom he had just glimpsed at the farther side of Death; God, whom modern society, with its ideas, its books and its teaching, had driven from his childish heart, and who now came back in spite of them all; that God of his mother whose Name he had once learned to pronounce, and who now returned within his soul and brought him to his knees in prayer.

O sweet recovered prayer, baby prayer learned years ago at a mother's knee, now arising anew within the heart, humble whisper óf love issuing from a meagre garret, lose not thy way, thou tiny column of incense, amid the uproar of the mighty city, but pass unsullied through the great dark cloud which hangs above the town, and rise pure white to heaven!

.   .   .   .   .   .

'Abel had recovered his faith. For some time past he had begun to frequent the "Patronage catholique," where he met other workmen who, like himself, were separated from their families and had come together and founded a new one. A priest was the affectionate and devoted father of this new and large family, whose members, actuated by similar needs and prompted by the same desires, met here to repair and rekindle their hearts by contact with the sublime Love; and here all these young men, worn out by the labours and the struggles of their daily life, came as often as they could to renew their spent forces in the struggle against their passions and against the world.

And Abel, as he watched these young men, their eyes aglow as they spoke of God, of virtue, of kindness to neighbours, of happiness for the people, bethought him of those others whom he had met so often in the cabaret, with their pale faces, their wrinkled lips, their eyes red with dissipation, who talked but of their vices, and discussed among themselves, in terms obscene, another love and another happiness—that of the egoist.

Here in the company of friends, where he felt nearer to God and learned to love and to defend his religion, Abel felt an apostolic desire growing in his workman's heart, the desire to make that religion known and loved. And this desire was not like others; for it troubled him not, but rather filled him with a sweet contentment.

He had informed his mother of the change that had taken place within him, and that he was now a frequenter of the "Patronage," and enjoyed being there; and she, much moved, had hastened to reply, telling him how glad she was and how happy his news had made her.

And he, too, was happy—this little apprentice. His was the real happiness, not that which wealth and honour may procure, and which ends with the tomb, but that which endures for ever, and which all, small and great, might own, did they but wish for it.

And the new light, in its infinite purity and brightness, which now enveloped Abel's soul and was destined to do so more and more, seemed somehow to dim the glory of his dream, cherished though it still was with the same affection and the same secret hope.

Dream on, little Abel! Let the bright image that thou hast created still charm thee as of yore; ravish thine eyes with its splendour while it still caresses thee, for the day will come when it will fade from thy sight, nor shall thine eyes descry it even through thy tears, though thou look for it as one searches for some beloved object for ever vanished from view!

Yet it was fair, thy childish dream; and generous, too, inspired by a mother's tears! So pure, so noble was it, that it filled thy heart almost before thou didst grasp its meaning, and when once thou didst seem to have fallen almost into an ecstasy, it was thy dream that was passing before thy wondering eyes.

Ah, yes! Thy dream was fair and noble,

and yet, little Abel, with thy generous heart, it was not great enough; and while thou didst spend thy days in pondering how best to fulfil it, God on his side was preparing thee another, still more unselfish, still more sublime, before whose brightness thine own was destined to grow pale indeed.

CHAPTER VI

GOD SPEAKS

ABEL'S employer, M. Moreau, had not failed to notice a considerable change in his apprentice.

"Well, it's not too soon," he remarked; "the lad seems no longer uninterested; the difficult time is over, and I think he'll stay with us now."

Ere long he learned the cause of the change, and that Abel went to church and attended the "Patronage," and although he was not, as he said, one of that sort himself, he was not unwilling to close his weather eye, for his custom was not to interfere with his work-people, especially when their personal habits did not clash with the business of the day.

The two mocking and sarcastic assistants, however, did not follow the example of their master in leaving Abel alone. On the contrary, they lost no chance of calling him *calotin*,[1] devotee, and so forth. However, he made as though he did not hear them, and retired more and more into himself.

One day, however, a violent discussion took place on the subject of the clergy. While Abel, carried away by his indignation, was defending them, one of the assistants said to him pointedly:

"If you are so fond of the curés, and are so good at defending them, why don't you give up all and become a priest?"

Strange to say, this remark, uttered ironically as it was, instead of irritating Abel as his interlocutor had expected, re-echoed in his innermost consciousness in a tone altogether different, producing a strange effect upon him, as if God had made use of the

---

[1] Clerical; literally, "lover of the biretta."

words as they fell from those mocking lips to call a soul.

"Leave all and become a priest!"

These words resounded gently in Abel's heart and moved him powerfully and sweetly. It was another voice than the mocking one which spake them.

Just at that moment a customer entered, and the two assistants paid no more attention to Abel, who had made no reply and stood pale and silent.

"Leave everything and become a priest, and be my apostle." They are always the same words, and they are always inspired by the same love, and it is always the same Voice which breathes them in the heart!

Since it sounded in Judea two thousand years ago, how many have heard it in the depths of their consciousness, in all its simplicity and love, speaking as it does especially to the humble, as it had just spoken to the little apprentice in the great city!

"Leave all and become a priest!"

He possessed nothing, this son of the poor widow, this little apprentice,—nothing but a dream, but it was such a beautiful dream! . . .

CHAPTER VII

THE TWO DREAMS

THE thought that he might become a priest filled Abel with a sudden and unknown joy, vibrating in all that was most tender and delicate in the secret recesses of his soul. When, however, he had well considered the sacrifice he was about to make, and had realized all that he must give up, he had hesitated. He would wait.

At last, one afternoon, when he was free to go out, he made up his mind to go and see the chaplain of the "Patronage," and to tell him everything and ask his advice. And now he had set out. The air was still, the sky cloudless, the streets almost silent. But what tumultuous thoughts coursed

70

through his brain; what agitation and trouble lay in his heart!

Before reaching the chaplain's quarters he entered a church to collect his thoughts. As he knelt there in the nave, alone, a strange contentment penetrated his inmost being. His eyes were drawn to the great crucifix where hung that pale and bleeding Victim who seemed to be mounting upwards from the altar in a perpetual self-oblation.

Then Abel's eyes returned to the tabernacle. He was there, then, in the little tabernacle, the Almighty God! Here in this church dwelt the God of Love—and the church was empty!

In the midst of the city, in the midst of the crowd which He so loved and on which He had once looked in such compassion, that Jesus who so loved it still dwelt—and the crowd outside passed by, indifferent, without one thought of His solitude. He

71

who alone could dry all tears, who alone could heal and strengthen, was here present before men's eyes, and the poor, the hopeless, the little ones, the vanquished in life's struggle, came not to Him!

He who would not leave us orphans was here in our midst, and He was abandoned! No heads were bowed in adoration, no hands joined in prayer, no hearts full of tenderness to satisfy His thirst for love!

Abel raised his eyes again towards Him whom all abandoned—towards the great Forsaken One of this age of ours. He encountered His inexplicable look, in which Eternal Love seems to blend with infinite suffering and immense compassion; and the longer he looked, the more the Figure seemed to lose the hard expression of pain, and as the expression softened it seemed to Abel that the softening was because of him, because he was showing pity. Then, moved to the depths of his being, Abel's heart went out towards this God who, suffering through love, seemed to force Himself by a love still greater, by a love more intimate, more tender, to forget His sorrows for an instant, and to suffer no longer in order that He might love the more. And in this supreme moment Abel made the great renunciation.

In place of those who no longer give God anything, he would give himself. He would be His apostle, to make Him better known; he would be among those who cry to the people as they point them to the crucifix: "Look and see if any one has loved thee as He has!"

He would be His priest; he would defend Him from His enemies; he would entice the crowd back to the churches, and bring men to their knees at the foot of the all-conquering Cross.

Before this great vision of the future, the former one which had so long charmed him grew pale. This new dream which he dreamed on his knees before the crucifix, beneath the small wan light in the sanctuary, blotted out the other which he had dreamed so often among the footpaths of his home, amid the flowers, the scents and the brilliant sunlight of springs long passed away. For that had been the somewhat selfish dream of the child who lived in a fairyland and knew nothing of life, whereas this new dream was the generous vision of the labourer already ripened by service and endurance. It was, too, the dream of youth disillusioned; youth who now sees things as they are, and who learns before the altar whereon the purest and most innocent Victim offers Himself, that there is something nobler than riches, fairer than honour, grander than glory—Sacrifice!

He would never be the celebrated man, the brilliant artist, the hero of dazzling successes, of whom he had so often dreamed, nor his mother the rich and happy lady of whom his childish mind had drawn so tender and caressing a picture.

No; neither fortune nor honour would be his, but poverty, contempt and maybe hatred. Instead of pleasure, he would have suffering, but he was in love with that suffering which had pierced the body and soul of a God, and by that holy contact, by that quasi-incarnation, had become forever divine.

Abel remained long on his knees before the great Christ, a humble image of sorrow adoring a greater sorrow still.

And at that moment his suffering and his love seemed to rise from his heart to the divine Crucified One, from him who was suffering himself to Him who had done so once for all, in the mounting of human love and sorrow towards a more sublime sorrow and a still greater love.

For it is in darkness and in silence, in

75

the fellowship of that wondrous reconcilia-
tion, in the mystery of that sublime inter-
course, that great transformations have their
birth, that deepest sorrows are changed
into transcendent joys and sacrifices are
consummated.

And it was here that Abel made his renunciation, one that his fellow men would
never know.

When he left the church all doubt and
hesitation had vanished. Jesus Christ the
Sufferer, Jesus Christ the Forsaken and the
Despised, had passed into his heart, and his
heart was no longer the same.

He sought out the chaplain and confided
to him his great desire to be a priest, speaking in terms so clear and unmistakable, and
in words so burning and sincere, that the
young priest, when Abel had departed,
could scarce restrain his tears. In those
days of persecution for the Church of
France, how many new and unexpected

apostles were hastening to her defence, and those who came were for the most part sons of the people, children of the working man!

They came, forsaking their callings, abandoning the position they had made in the world, in order to take the places of those other privileged ones who, first chosen, surrounded by every care, and prepared through long years of study, had renounced their vocation, some of them shamefully betraying their trust, and opposing all that they had sworn to defend, becoming the persecutors of those who had brought them up.

The chaplain turned his eyes to the crucifix, towards Him who, in spite of traitors and enemies, can always find enough courage and fidelity in the hearts of the people to console Him for the evil that men do to Him; towards that Jesus who at the moments of supreme crisis loves to choose His defenders among the humble, for they betray not, and when they give themselves they do so entirely and forever.

The soul of the priest, strengthened as it were by contact with the fresh young soul of the boy, recovered its force, and as he took up his pen he felt his faith grow stronger and his hope more certain.

.   .   .   .   .   .

When Abel descended from his room at six o'clock to resume his duties, he held in his hand a letter for his mother. His fingers gripped the letter feverishly, for that little white envelope contained the new secret of his life and his future.

To-morrow his new dream would be revealed, and the old one would be thrust back into the innermost recesses of his heart, where no man should ever know of its existence.

CHAPTER VIII

A MOTHER'S SACRIFICE

MME. VERDIER received her son's letter with considerable surprise and some emotion, for the sudden decision which it contained changed once and for all the future to which she had hitherto looked forward.

And this hesitation was mingled with a certain sense of fear, for she knew the society in which she lived, and by means of which she earned her daily bread. She knew its passions and its hatreds, and could gauge better than any one else the point to which its hardness and tyrannical want of pity might extend against those who resisted it. She knew, too, how much suffer-

79

ing it was able to inflict. And she could
not forget that in these days there is one
thing which especially excites its hate, and
which it never pardons.

She foresaw what people would say.; the
struggles which she would have to undergo
in a community where unbelief and contempt for religion reign unchallenged, and
where true charity has been replaced by a
pseudo-fraternity.

She foresaw the shipwreck of all the
secret hopes she had formed for her son,
with his talent and passionate love for the
violin.

Yes; all these thoughts assailed Abel's
mother, but while the great ladies of the
world, with their wealth and independence,
too often refuse their sons to God, she, the
poor grocer, the fortuneless widow who regarded the future with fear, and foresaw
the struggles she must undergo, never hesitated, but freely surrendered to Him her

beloved Abel. What matter what the world might say or do, the world which is full of jealousy and hatred of the weak, and of the poor who do their duty and make their sacrifice? What matter, since it was for God?

CHAPTER IX

THE LAST VIOLIN LESSON

ON Wednesday, a few days after his interview with the chaplain, Abel went as usual to his violin lesson.

Never before had he paid so much attention; never before had he played with such *élan* as he did during this lesson. It seemed as if he wished it to serve for all the lessons which he would have to relinquish in future.

He reserved all his powers for the last piece he played, and threw his whole soul into the music, as if wishing to show all his talent on the last occasion that he would play to his master.

The piece, a veritable swan-song, seemed a long and melodious sigh in which the young artist wept for his art and said a last farewell to renown.

For Abel, the little fiddler, who had dreamt of such brilliant successes and had desired human praise with all his heart, longing some day to play before the great ones of this world, would henceforth play for himself alone.

When the lesson was ended, the professor with cruel and unconscious irony praised his playing in terms more emphatic than he had ever employed before.

"Poor Père Choutot!" thought Abel as he said good-bye; "if he knew that this perhaps is my last lesson!"

He left the house, pressing his black case closer than ever under his left arm.

"My last lesson!"

He could not reconcile himself to the idea, and yet it was true that he could not continue them. That he understood. Henceforth he could not add that expense

to so many other indispensable ones.
He would have a *bourse*—a scholarship—
it is true; the chaplain had promised
that, but his mother would be obliged to
buy him his dress, to pay for his books and
papers, and all the various articles necessary for his studies.

His last lesson!

He walked on, absorbed and sad, bear-
ing in his heart all the bitterness of those
three words. He walked on, scarcely seeing the various people whom he passed,
his eyes fixed on something that no one
could see and which was fading forever
from his eyes,—the image of his vanished
dream.

O you rich children with teachers to in-
struct you in all the arts and all the sci-
ences; you on whom lessons of all sorts are
squandered, and who don't even know the
cost of them; children or youths whom
study wearies and who often complain of

being compelled to learn, making those who surround you pay dearly for your occasional attention and your slow progress; how will you ever know what sad regret and what bitter longing lie hidden in those words:

"My last lesson!"

Never will you know what it costs to say: "Here my knowledge must end; I may not go any further. The page I have just read is the end of the book for me! All the leaves which come afterwards, and which I turn over longingly, must remain unknown. They are reserved for others who have the means to learn, who can continue to improve in their art, while I must learn to forget mine."

Abel was walking down an avenue enclosed on each side by noble chestnut trees whose thick foliage met above his head, mingling together to afford him greater coolness and shade.

He felt that shade and that coolness as they sank upon him like a wave of sweet forgetfulness. Looking up, he saw here and there in the foliage traces of yellow tints which were beginning to replace the green.

Autumn had come!

CHAPTER X

THE RETORT

WHEN Abel returned home he found the letter he was expecting from his mother, who, while expressing her surprise, welcomed his decision with tender emotion, encouraging him in his resolution and announcing that she would arrive on the morrow to take him away.

So he would not remain here even a day longer!

He could not inform his master, for the latter was away, and would not be back till very late that night.

Abel returned to his work, filled with a new and unknown joy. That evening there were many customers in M. Moreau's saloon; people of all conditions of life. Abel knew many of them who had been regular customers during the three months that he had been there, and although most of them had never spoken a word to him, nevertheless he was sorry to leave them.

Those whom he regretted most were the working men who came of an evening after leaving their workshops, and to whose complaints, revolts, and occasional blasphemies he had often listened, but whom he could not help loving on account of their hard life.

He pitied them as he thought that they would continue to come with the same tired eyes, the same distrustful expression, the same sighs and sad words on their lips.

Yes, he was sorry indeed for these men who did not understand the true cause of their trouble, and who perchance would never know the truth.

He felt a melancholy regret when he

thought that he, a working man like themselves, who might listen to them and talk naturally with them, was going away without being able to leave behind him even a shred of that truth which sustained him, not a drop of that love which overflowed in his boyish heart.

While Abel was indulging in these thoughts, a small, thin man of about fifty came in, smiling, holding between his fingers a newspaper which he had just bought from the paper-boy whose voice was heard receding in the distance.

The new arrival was an habitué. He took off his greatcoat with much ceremony, hung it on its accustomed peg, and then, adjusting his yellow pince-nez on his nose, screwing up his eyes as he surveyed the other visitors to the establishment who had the honour of being in his presence, he sat down, opened his newspaper as wide as possible, and placed it on his knees.

Abel knew this man well—better, in fact, than the others. He had seen him four times a week during the last four months; but although he had seen him often, Abel had never been able to grow accustomed to his presence. Every time that he saw him at the entrance to the doorway he could scarce restrain a frown and a gesture of annoyance. He experienced a positive repulsion for this little pedantic and affected schoolmaster, with his look of sublime self-sufficiency and the contemptuous and satisfied smile which always lurked in the corners of his mouth.

Yes; from the moment that he appeared, Abel's whole being rebelled against this affected and contemptuous functionary, small of heart and narrow of intellect, who had ever on his tongue the words "people," "fraternity," "philanthropy," while he tormented the attendants with his requirements and his fussy caprices. The napkins were never sufficiently white for him, nor the razor blades sufficiently sharp. The assistant's fingers, too, were never clean nor soft enough when they came in contact with Monsieur's delicate skin; while, on the other hand, the little silver money-box was too deep and too vast to receive the sou which on rare occasions he dropped ostentatiously into it.

Ever since Abel had known this pedagogue-politician, with his ferocious anti-clericalism and his incorrigible habit of commenting on all the principal articles in the papers, he had noticed how the man's lips opened and contracted as his thick moustache rubbed against his nose, while he emitted insults and invectives against the Church and her priests.

His favourite words were "curé," "calotin," "Jesuit," which he rolled unctuously over his tongue, as if to soil them the more in his contempt.

No; Abel certainly would not regret *him!*

As he ran his razor backwards and forwards over the black, shiny strop, Abel looked at the man in the glass and saw a line of large letters which ran across his newspaper. Perplexed at what he saw, he drew back a step or two, and before taking his place behind his customer, preparatory to beginning to shave him, he threw a rapid and furtive glance at the paper. The black, sinister lines seemed to pierce his half-closed eyes and to strike his heart with a savage blow. This is what he read:

"The Concordat torn up! Clericalism defeated!"

When Abel began to run his razor over the white lather his hand trembled.

Complete silence reigned in the room; nothing was to be heard but the slight whistling of the razors as they passed over the skin, removing the beard with a scraping sound.

Soon, however, the silence was broken by the small, piercing voice of the schoolmaster, and Abel grew sick at heart as he heard the well-known sound. It rose, insinuating and hard, like the hiss of a serpent.

"The separation is voted, and none too soon! The bishops may shake their mitres and brandish their croziers as much as they please to anathematize us, but they won't prevent the death of the Church which they boasted to be immortal! Eh, gentlemen?"

There was a murmur of vague assent. Some of the company, working men mostly, turned attentively towards the speaker, while others continued reading their papers without moving, or looked up indifferently at the ceiling.

"She is long-lived, the Church," said some one.

"I bet she recovers," said the coarse voice of a workman, drawn out of his silence by this conversation.

Abel appeared to be indifferent. The two assistants, who were watching him to note what effect had been produced upon him, were surprised at his calmness.

After a pause the schoolmaster continued with increased sarcasm:

"Now they can tighten their belts at their ease, the rats! That won't cause them any difficulty, for they have plenty of girth. However, as they won't want to die of hunger, they'll soon have to capitulate and clear out altogether. If by chance they prove obstinate, I should be inclined, and it would be quite legal, to make them pay the patent tax, like charlatans. We've given them money enough; they can well afford to give us some in their turn."

On finishing this long sentence, the little schoolmaster cast a circular gaze round the room, to mark the effect of his speech and to note any smiles of approval.

These insulting words, which no one took up, not even the two gentlemen whom Abel had often seen at church, made his young blood boil. The colour rose to his face as he felt the eyes of the two assistants fixed upon him, as if to excite him and to emphasize the sarcasm. It was too much for him, and he replied:

"How much money have you ever given the clergy, Monsieur,—you who are asking your money back?"

There was a moment of silence. All eyes were raised and fixed on the young man who stood there quivering. The schoolmaster's eyes lit up with an evil light.

What! This boy, this ignoramus, joining in the discussion and daring to answer him!

He looked Abel up and down contemptuously.

"Young man, I should be ashamed to have given them a single sou in all my life."

"Then why do you say, 'We have given them money enough'; and why do you talk of making them pay for it?"

"Because they are humbugs and ought to be made to pay a license before exercising their trade. That is the law."

The voice which replied grew more aggressive.

"It is against the law to insult other people. Prove that they are charlatans. We judge trees by their fruit, and men by their deeds. Those who teach a false and mutilated morality, promising to give to society model men and remarkable citizens, and who have produced nought but sceptics and hooligans,—those are the veritable charlatans of to-day, and God knows we pay for them dearly!"

The small, clear, resonant voice contrasted strongly with that of the schoolmaster. It penetrated deep into the hearts of the astonished hearers, and especially into those of the artisans.

Their faces, rendered ugly by hatred and hardness, grew softer; a trace of gentleness and sympathy passed over their features and lurked in their eyes,—those eyes which a single dangerous word can inflame or a single gentle one soften, eyes where hate does not really dwell, but always a vague longing to know and to believe.

The schoolmaster rose, furious and crimson in the face, crumpling up his paper in one hand while he gesticulated with the other.

"We believe what *we* teach, while the clergy don't believe a word of the stories they tell us. They deceive the people, and only think of gaining money."

"That is why they are so rich, I suppose," replied Abel ironically. "Tell me, Monsieur, if they stopped your salary to-day, would you teach in the school to-morrow? I think not. Very well; you will see whether the clergy, who only wish to get money, will give up their work because the State ceases to pay them."

In the silence which followed a thrill passed over the rude audience, as if the youthful force and generous excitement of the boy had entered into them, bringing with it, perhaps, some echo of the faith which transfigured Abel.

"We shall see," said the schoolmaster in a hollow voice. "Besides, even if they showed obstinacy, their day is sealed, they are powerless. Who do you think is sufficiently enthusiastic and sufficiently wanting in common sense to join them under present conditions?"

"I am, Monsieur," interrupted Abel, proudly, as a smile of joy and triumph lit up his features. "I enter the seminary to-morrow. So you see I, for my part, am not disposed to surrender."

The two assistants looked at each other, dumfounded.

"Not surprising," grumbled the little schoolmaster, taken aback. He sat down again, inwardly furious that he, the free-thinker before whom all trembled, before whose scepticism all convictions vanished, should have been stood up to and defeated by a young apprentice.

The working men regarded the school-master with changed expressions. They felt now a sort of contempt and disgust for the little functionary, with his evil face. But when they looked at Abel their expression was different, and they regarded him with a sort of sympathetic admiration. The former they knew well; he was the politician of the day. They had seen often enough the cruel, hypocritical smile on his lips, the sinister light in his eyes; they had heard before the blasphemies and the insults he had just given voice to, and they were tired of listening to them. Abel, on the other hand, was new to them. Without anger and without abuse, he had spoken in an unaccustomed voice, using words so sincere that they must be true. Then again, the other was a functionary, a *bourgeois,* whereas Abel was a working man like themselves.

For the first time these men, accustomed to hear all sorts of objections and invectives against religion, had heard a voice which answered those objections and demolished them, and they liked to listen to it.

They continued to gaze obstinately at the schoolmaster and the apprentice, and maybe they thought:

"That man in a few years will be living on his income in selfish comfort, while this youngster will be found bravely fighting in the midst of the battle, working amid hate, contempt, calumny and persecution, and when he grows old he may die of hunger.

Then they felt for him that same pity which he had felt for them,—pity for this child of the people who was devoting and sacrificing himself, and whom they perchance would themselves insult one day.

Yes; they seemed to feel pity and remorse, and to be asking themselves whether their teachers had not deceived them.

CHAPTER XI

THE VOICE FROM BENEATH

THAT night, when the shop was shut, Abel went up to his room while his comrades were getting ready to go out into the town. He was very tired, but before going to bed he leaned against the window-sill and looked out over the dark, confused masses of roofs growing less and less visible in the darkness. Then he looked down at the street where the pale light of the gas-lamps seemed to be struggling faintly with the shadows.

This was the last night that he would pass here.

To-morrow he would be far from this town, far from the world, from that hard, cruel world which had already made him suffer, and which he forgave, although he knew that it had other trials in store for him.

Yes; he forgave it, for was it not in order to work for the conversion of that world, was it not in order to give love in return for its hate, that he was leaving the honours that awaited him in his art?

Down in the street a far-away call, which seemed approaching nearer and nearer, caught his ear. Abel listened.

"Separation of Church and State!"

This sensational announcement, heralded through the night by a small, persistent voice, re-echoed strangely in his heart. To him that voice was not merely that of the newsboy, it was that of the town itself repeating the phrase of the day in one ironical farewell.

At that hour this same cry would be rising from thousands of similar voices in every corner of France. And Abel thought he heard them all announcing the official apostasy of a nation.

And amid all these vile rumours of hatred which seemed to resound from every side, he felt a deeper and more tender affection for Him who was being denied.

But now, amid these voices, others began to rise—not official these, but more natural, more spontaneous, more ancient voices which for centuries past have risen up each evening at the hour of the "Ave."

Upwards they rose, and Abel heard them, and it seemed to him that they softened, dominated and extinguished the others. And they seemed to him like an unanimous murmur of faith, troth and love rising out of the old soil of France to disown the raucous voices of hatred and denial.

Carried away by the impression, he mingled his voice with those voices of prayer as they cried for pardon on the world, and with tears in his eyes he gazed upward toward that great heaven which listens to the feeble whispers of men, to their praises and to their blasphemies; and it seemed to him as he did so, that from the myriads of stars whose eyes gazed down on the earth there fell that night one mighty glance of compassion.

CHAPTER XII

LAST VISIONS—LAST TEARS

THE express carried Abel and his mother far from the town where he had lived for the last four months.

He watched it gradually vanish, that town where he and so many others had suffered; where he had learned better to understand what life is; where God, whom he had forgotten, had come to seek him; where in one day all his ravishing illusions had vanished, and where in so short a time he had grown from a child into a man.

And as he watched that dark object growing less and less and finally disappear on the horizon, it was not only the flying shadow of a city that he saw, but the last shadow of the past, the farewell vision of his dream.

Soon he could see no more. All had disappeared. Then tears rose in his eyes—tears of hidden suffering.

O Thou who once didst bless tears; Christ, who didst come on earth to weep, how precious must those tears have been to Thee—a thousand times more precious than pearls! With what love didst Thou gather them, those tears which a child-apostle shed in one last look back at what he had relinquished to follow Thee!

"How sensitive he is!" thought Mme. Verdier as she watched him. Poor Mother! If she had known!

CHAPTER XIII

WHAT WILL THE WORLD SAY?

TWO travellers—Mme. Verdier and her son—stood before the great door of the seminary.

They looked for a moment at the beautiful open belfry which rose above the surrounding buildings, as the rays of the sun gilded it with dazzling light. Then Abel pulled the copper bell-pull with a hand that trembled slightly.

A door opened wide in front of them.

The first thing they saw as they entered was the white statue of the Virgin standing out amid the golden foliage. She was close to them, with her gentle smile of infinite tenderness. It did their eyes and

108

their hearts good, and rewarded them for all they had suffered. For Abel especially, on the threshold of his new home, the figure seemed a ray of sunlight and of divine hope which entered into his heart, just as it had said farewell for ever to all earthly light and happiness.

The porter led them to the Superior, whose fatherly kindness and tender good humour rejoiced the hearts of these humble ones, accustomed as they were to the rudeness of the world.

After questioning them both, the Superior gazed long at the mother and son. He had before him the orphan and the widow of a working man, and the old priest, who had seen many sacrifices, knew that this one was greater than the others. He began to speak to them as a father does to his children. At times his voice had so penetrating an accent, and said so many tender things, that Mme. Verdier felt the tears in her eyes; then he grew animated, and his words inflamed Abel's heart and brought before his eyes another dream, that great one which, once seen, had replaced the old one, and which would be with him all his life long.

Mme. Verdier quitted the seminary feeling stronger and more confident, and her heart was filled with an unknown joy.

Yet this peace, so tranquil and serene, which she bore away with her from that saintly abode, was from time to time troubled by a persistent question which she had never dared to face, but which she foresaw with anguish notwithstanding.

What would the world say?

Abel, who watched her departure, but knew not her anxiety, put up this prayer for her in his heart:

"O God, give her a little of that happiness which I dreamed I could give her one day!"

THE TWO DREAMS

PART II

CHAPTER I

ON THE HILLSIDE

THE group of young students—about forty boys in all—welcomed Abel with open arms. He appeared to them a recruit sent by Providence, this new arrival who seemed already old to his comrades, although he was scarcely fifteen. One soon grows old in the world.

But here he was destined to find again the affection and kindness of which he had been deprived, and they gradually transformed him. Just as a flower opens better in the warm light which makes its life, so his nature, which the world had rendered shy and self-contained, now began to open again in this atmosphere of goodness, and

113

to unfold gradually and naturally in this unknown and supernatural light.

A few days after his arrival they all went for a walk. As they climbed a steep hill, they saw the city below them descending as they ascended, shrinking away into the hollows like a huge block of stone which has become detached from the hillside, and, rolling down into the valley, has been long worked and chiselled into shape with incredible patience. And the valley, with its yellow autumn tints, seemed like a gigantic golden casket which enclosed this block of precious stone.

Abel gazed for some time at the long silver riband which glittered down in the plain; for it was his river, the Yonne, the river of his home, and it came from over yonder, whence he came also. He followed the course of the river back and back as far as he could see, and then his eyes rested on the dark hills silhouetted in the distance, then they pierced to the line of the horizon and centred on a spot scarcely visible in the sky which he saw in imagination as it opened to reveal still more distant horizons. And beyond these imaginary horizons he seemed to distinguish a point invisible to the eye, and thought:

"That's where I was yesterday."

Ere long he ceased to gaze at these far distances, and grew to watching the leaves as they fell in melancholy grace all round him. One by one, yellowed by age, they dropped quietly from their branches, began slowly turning round, gliding obliquely to the right or the left, poised for a moment in mid-air as if filled with a sort of regret, and then, as if to lengthen their fall, letting themselves be carried hither and thither until they sank to the ground, dead once and for all.

And every time a puff of wind passed

over them, more of these poor leaves fell in a cascade of gold.

Abel watched this breath of decay which caused the landscape to shiver as it passed over it, drawing from it at each moment a further portion of its life; and as he watched he thought of death, whose grandiose and striking image lay spread out before his eyes.

He seemed to see death poised over a dying nature from whom the sun seemed to have withdrawn for ever. He saw it in the slow and melancholy fall of the leaves, and in that yellow tint which it throws over all beings and all things when it causes them to perish.

And as he watched this death which had so frightened him recently, and which he had regarded with so much terror, he found that the thought no longer troubled him, but now filled him with gentle calm. He loved now to listen to the sigh which it drew from everything, and to bathe his eyes and his soul in its monotonous and soothing colouring.

And the spectacle of nature dying in order to be born again into a richer and fuller life taught him that man must face death not once only, in order to receive another life, but many times, dying to himself, to his desires, his hopes and his dreams, to arise to nobler and more certain visions.

CHAPTER II

A CHANGED VILLAGE

THE fears which Mme. Verdier had felt at the bottom of her heart when she learned the sudden decision of her son, proved only too well founded. In spite of its old-fashioned appearance, Vally was a modern village.

The traveller, as he passed along the highroad from Paris and saw it at the end of its delicious valley embowered in verdure, a very poem of quiet and restful simplicity, with its houses lovingly clustered round its church, was wont to think:

"How I should like to rest here! How sweet to live in this peaceful village, far from the fratricidal strife of party; from

the hideous passions and criminal hatreds
of political life! How good to rest awhile
beneath the shadow of that ancient church,
where love must come naturally to all, and
where one can taste the innocent joys of
the good old days!"

Alas! how soon he would have been disillusioned if he had absently strayed from
the highroad and turned down the narrow
path leading to the village! With what
astonishment would he have passed by those
broken crosses, and how hardly he would
have recognized in those men, with their
hard, malevolent faces bending spitefully
over the ground, continuing their work and
even their oaths while the "Angelus"
sounded above them, the happy peasants of
simple faith that his imagination had pictured!

And if he had approached the church,
that ancient church which from afar seemed
sustained, as it were, by the love of the vil-

lage, he would have discovered to his dismay that it no longer formed part of the village life. It was deserted, and its cracked walls and dilapidated arches gave it the appearance of some poor old granddame neglected by all and weeping over her children's forgetfulness.

For the church at Vally, like so many of our small parish churches in France, resembled a body from which the life and the soul have departed. For what is a church's soul? Surely it is that of her people, which fills her, sustaining her with their prayers; the soul, trembling within her, of a people living their joys and their sorrows within her walls, and making her live with their life.

This soul had fled, and the poor church had fallen into ruin. Every Sunday a priest from the neighbouring village still came to say Mass, but only for some twenty persons, nearly all of them old women.

The Church had nothing left her but what remained to her out of the past.

Those who once had filled the now empty benches, mingling their prayers and their chants, their joys and their sorrows, in a brotherly union blessed by God, were now dead. They were all gone from this world, those old peasants, those true friends and maintainers of the soil, who represented it, who defended it everywhere, and especially in church, where they prayed for it.

Aye, they prayed for it. To-day their successors pray no more for the land; they do not even hear the soft murmur of the "Angelus," which once caused their forbears, whom nothing else could stay, to cease their work when they heard those bells, and to turn in meditation towards the far-off tower. Then, at that moment when all the plain was silent, something moving, mysterious, would arise from the furrows beneath their feet, transfiguring them and making them tremble, as the warm, palpitating soil of their native earth, the soil of their beloved fatherland, joined with their spirits in prayer.

Yes; they were all gone, those old peasants; and those who had filled their places at the fireside and in the fields had left their seats in church empty and void. For the sons of the old people, glad enough to inherit their material possessions, had rejected their moral ones; they took over their fathers' cottages and acres, but not their habits, their beliefs and their hopes.

They had a noble and ancient heritage, but would take only the poorest part of it, preferring the cold egotism and implacable hardness of the sceptic to the tender pity and holy charity of their ancestors. They had replaced love by hatred,—hatred which divided them in everything but in their hostility to the God who had united their fathers, and who would still unite themselves even in their accursed revolt against Him.

"Where are our sons who should take our place on the earth?" This must be the cry of those old labourers and husbandmen of former days, if at times on Sundays they revisit the little village church with its countless empty benches.

CHAPTER III

HATRED AT WORK

IT was about three months after Abel entered the seminary when the news began to spread in his native village, where it was thought that he was still serving his apprenticeship.

Some were astonished and others angry; few were indifferent. Now that something was known, Mme. Verdier was overwhelmed with questions.

"Where did your son get the idea? Didn't he like his work?"

"Why didn't you dissuade him? He doesn't know the future that awaits him. He will die of hunger, now that the clergy are no longer paid. That trade was right enough in the past, but to-day——"

"My poor woman," said others, with a pity which appeared sincere, "that boy of yours will be a trouble to you."

These were the remarks constantly reiterated, which the poor woman had to listen to all day long, and to which she had to reply.

All these conversations in the shop and during her journeys through the parish came back to her at night when she was alone, and caused her a sort of indefinable discomfort in which anxiety played a considerable part. She felt herself at the mercy of these hard, unbelieving people, who loved to make others suffer, and she feared for the future.

As soon as they had heard the news, all the bigoted anti-clericals closed their doors to the little itinerant grocer. Nor was she surprised thereat; indeed, she had expected it.

If her affairs remained at that, it would

only make the difference of some thirty persons out of an average of one hundred and fifty. The loss was not very great. She would not die of hunger in consequence.

Thus she consoled herself. But one night very late, when she had just finished her preparations for her morning's rounds, she was surprised to see enter her shop one of the customers who had left her.

He was a man of about fifty, whose small frigid face seemed to be hiding itself behind his long grey beard. Not much was known of this retired functionary, whose proceedings were wrapped in mystery, except that he was anti-clerical and held advanced opinions.

During the five or six years that he had lived at Vally, he had obtained a dangerous influence over his neighbours. The civil authorities secretly obeyed him, and even those who professed independence feared

126

him, for, in the popular language, "he had a long arm."

As a matter of fact, he had found good places for several persons, and he was feared because people might have need of his influence.

Mme. Verdier came forward to ask what he wanted.

He began in a cold, solemn tone which he intended to be imposing.

"Madame," he said, "I have come to-day, entirely in your interest, to talk to you of serious matters regarding your son who is at the seminary."

"About my son at the seminary?" repeated Mme. Verdier, blankly. "And what do you want with my son?" she asked, knowing beforehand what he would say.

"I have nothing to say to him, for he is only a child; but I ask you, Madame, to bring him to reason."

The hard, authoritative voice now grew mild and gentle.

"Understand me, dear Madame, I beg. You have an excellent clientèle, and if you want to keep it you must humour it. It would be a tactless thing to go against the ideas of your customers."

"Pardon, Monsieur; I respect the ideas of others, and all I ask is that my own and those of my son may be respected also."

"But in placing your son in the seminary you are combating the opinions of the district from which you draw your livelihood, and upon which you are consequently dependent."

"Then you would like me to force my son to quit the seminary?"

"Naturally, Madame. I shall make it my business to find him a good post."

Mme. Verdier went on, without listening to him:

"You wish me to make use of my power

128

over him to compel him! That is a thing I shall never do, Monsieur. Do you understand?"

There was anger in her voice. She was a mother, and she could defend her child.

The man changed colour slightly, and there was a moment of silence while he seemed to be trying to regain his self-control. Then he replied coldly, in a hard, quiet voice:

"You forget, Madame, that it is in your own interest that I have come to see you this evening, and you make a great mistake in showing useless annoyance. It will be greatly to your advantage to listen to me and to think the matter over. Time presses, but I am willing to wait two days before I return to receive your definite answer."

So they were trying to frighten her, because she was a poor woman, and were pretending to hold a pistol to her head. She must show this man who was trying to intimidate her that she was not afraid of him.

"It is useless to give me time," she replied. "My answer would be the same; I shall never consent to do what you ask!"

"Don't irritate me, Madame; and remember for the last time that you must have bread to eat."

"I would sooner die, Monsieur, than eat your bread. It costs too dear."

The man turned pale, and retired to the door, lashed by the small, quivering voice. Before opening it, however, he muttered these words to the poor woman, accompanying them by a look of hatred which struck at her heart and left her trembling:

"You don't know me yet, miserable woman, but soon you will regret your words, when it is too late!"

Then he took his departure.

The man walked away alone into the darkness, full of thoughts of vengeance. He continued his walk for some time.

Arriving at length in an unfrequented alley, he halted before a window through whose closed shutters a ray of light appeared, and knocked several times on the door.

"Is that you?" asked a smothered voice from within.

The man made some answer, and disappeared through a door which was silently opened to admit him.

Above, the moon shed her pale light upon the house, as if to try and dispel its mystery and to penetrate its shadows and the secrecy which concealed the labour of hate.

There were six men together, and they were discussing how best to snatch the bread from the mouth of one poor widow who had dared to resist them, and who was praying alone in her room, her tear-dimmed eyes resting upon the crucifix.

Talk, consult together, you, whoever you

are, who are accustomed to meet in that dark dwelling. Turn over in your minds the dark designs which to-morrow will be accomplished! Plot the most hideous and cowardly of all plots, that against a poor, defenceless woman; and beware, mysterious plotters, and hide yourselves in the darkness, and speak with bated breath, lest bye and bye your dangerous enemy, that poor, weeping woman, should hear you,— for then . . . Poor men!

CHAPTER IV

ALONE AGAINST THE WORLD

IN the course of several months since the secret hate had begun its work, the little grocer at the corner, as she was called, had lost many of her customers, and every day she lost more.

Each morning, on her rounds through the parish, she found doors closed against her which yesterday had been open.

Now, when she entered her customers' doors, it was with a feeling of fear and anxiety. She saw on their faces before they spoke what they were going to say. And even if they received her kindly she would say to herself as she left:

"This is perhaps the last time that I shall call here!"

Some people stopped her by saying roughly, "It is useless to come back; we sha'n't buy anything more from you." Others, less daring, simply kept their doors closed. Then she would call there two or maybe three more days, but after that she no longer dared, and passed timidly on behind her cart. Those who used to buy much from her had only to say, "I don't want anything." She knew what that meant, and went more sadly on her way, knowing that her enemies had been there before her.

And now that they were determined to take all her customers from her, Mme. Verdier called scarcely anywhere, but passed on, bending wearily over her little tradesman's cart. She traversed the streets of the village timidly and resignedly, often without turning her head, past two long rows of doors which opened no longer to the sound of her bell; and as she passed, she felt the

134

eyes of the neighbours spying at her from behind their curtains, and she hurried on out of range of those pitiless eyes.

Every day she returned from her rounds more uneasy, more tired, and with the greater part of her goods unsold.

And at home she was careful not to complain before her old mother or her little Joel; for the one was too old, and the other too young, and she wished to spare them. Abel, too, she would spare, if possible, and she had told him nothing of what was happening.

"What is the good of discouraging them and making them suffer before they must?" she would often say to herself.

But at night, when she was alone, she would cry softly, feeling the weight of the hatred which overwhelmed her, and praying to God to support her.

Her enemies directed the attack with method and ability. First it was the government officials, then the tradespeople, whom they turned against her; then the more or less independent working men, and finally the peasantry who were freethinkers or indifferent or hostile to religion. At last they approached the poor who were in receipt of parish relief, and even threatened to withdraw their allowance if they dared to deal with Mme. Verdier.

A heart-breaking spectacle, that of six men furiously exerting every interest, every passion, every hatred against one poor woman! Every day Mme. Verdier felt herself more and more forsaken, more and more cast out like a stranger.

Even among the customers who remained to her, those who dared to come to the shop were few. indeed. They were afraid to compromise themselves, and so all the noise and bustle which had formed part of her life seemed to have quit the little shop forever.

The shop-bell, which formerly knew scarcely an instant of repose, now slept peacefully and silently in its corner near the ceiling. The coffee-mill, formerly turned all day long by the small, nervous hands of its mistress, now remained motionless for long hours at a stretch; and Mme. Verdier, alone in her shop, surrounded by her stores which never grew less, sat behind her desk, pale and thin, her eyes lost in a vision of sorrow, awaiting the customers who never came.

Still she waited for them, and when on rare occasions the bell rang, and the welcome sound, now so rare, raised a sudden hope in her breast, and a customer entered, her lips bore a poor, sad smile of gratitude, as if to say: "Thank you for having had pity!"

Ah! how sad they were, those days passed in waiting, while she tried to fathom the reason for all this hate, asking herself whether, one day, when they thought she had suffered enough and wept enough, they would have pity, or whether there was no more hope, and all must end, and she must close the shop and leave this village, which rejected her, for ever.

And at times she suffered still more, fearing lest they should come and seize her goods. For some months past her stores had not been sold, and the drafts had come in at the usual dates. She had settled many of them, but two rather large ones remained in arrear, one for two hundred francs and the other for five hundred. She had begun by asking for two months' grace; then for another, hoping that times would change. And now the last fortnight of July was drawing to its close, and matters were going from bad to worse.

Formerly the wholesale people had been less impatient, but now one could see by their letters that they too had been subjected to the secret influence of the same pitiless hatred.

In a week's time some brokers would probably come from the town and liquidate her stock. It would be sold at absurdly low prices to those who had so long refused to buy from her, and then her enemies would be able to enjoy their vengeance to the full.

The poor woman nursed these fears until each day carried off with it a little more of her strength and tenacity of purpose. Still she continued to struggle, strong in her Christian faith and in her maternal affection, refusing to despair, unwilling to confess herself conquered.

For some time past she had thought of borrowing the necessary sum from a rich bourgeois family whom she still counted among her best remaining customers, but her natural pride and disinclination to owe anything to any one, and her fear of asking for anything, had made her put the idea aside. Now, however, she realized that she had no alternative, and she resolved to have recourse to this final means of obtaining assistance.

CHAPTER V.

THE LAST ROUND

THE clock was striking eight, and Mme. Verdier descended the high-street of the village, as she did every morning, pushing before her the little rumbling barrow.

She was walking sadly, with an overburdened air, but enveloped notwithstanding in a gentle light, the image of resigned sorrow.

The passers-by looked at her in surprise and disdain.

"Where can she be going?" they asked themselves; "who can there be who still buys from her?"

And she, instinctively divining their thoughts and their questions, asked herself:

"Why have I come?"

Aye, why had she come? Why did she
still move about with her wares? Would
she not have done better to stay at home,
out of the way of the scoffers? Ah! but she
still hoped.

She hoped that hatred would melt into
pity, and that the numberless doors now
shut would reopen, and she would forgive.

Mme. Verdier left several streets where
she no longer had any customers, and
sought those which still received her.
Many people who no longer liked to look
through her wares, bought them from her
in secret.

When she arrived before the rich bourgeois house where she was still received,
her heart beat faster. For the first time in
her life she was going to ask a loan, and
after having taken so long to make up her
mind, she now at the last moment hesitated.
Then the thought came to her of what

142

would happen if she didn't ask for help, and her fears vanished as she boldly rang the bell.

A servant appeared.

"Madame does not want anything, and has told me to say that she won't want anything in future."

The final words were said in a low voice, and in a tone as if the speaker, in repeating them, sought in pity to soften their hardness so as not too deeply to wound the heart of the poor woman.

Mme. Verdier grew deadly pale at this new and unexpected blow which shattered her last hope, and she stood there stupefied, immovable, while the door closed in her face. Then, remembering that she was probably being watched, she was seized with a sudden shame, and turning round mechanically, stumbled towards her barrow as if about to fall; and without glancing back she continued her journey, looking weaker, thinner, more despairing than ever.

Behind the window the maid-servant watched her through a gap in the curtain, as the poor woman went away, bent beneath the blow, and the girl, having a simple heart wherein no hatred found a place, was seized with pity, and turned from the window with tears in her eyes.

Mme. Verdier hurried homewards in order to shut herself in. A few days more, and the brokers would come in. She had finished her last round. Now she must leave the neighbourhood, and who could tell whether the hatred of her enemies might not follow her? As she thought over these things, her soul was filled with anguish.

For a long time past she had scarcely slept, and her strength, which she had never husbanded, had become exhausted, and her health had suffered; and now, beneath an

144

appearance of pallor, she was consumed by a hidden fever and shaken by an ague.

Was she going to be ill? The idea terrified her, and she hurried her pace as if to escape from the sickness within her.

All at once, as she passed before the house of her chief enemy, the man who had paid her that nocturnal visit which had brought her all her trouble, she heard a well-known voice which made her tremble.

"There she is!" it cried.

She knew that some one was pointing her out, and she drew herself up, lest her enemies with the hate in their eyes should see her suffering. There were two up there who were looking down at her. A diabolical joy lit up their eyes and spread over their features in a hideous smile, as they saw in that poor face, withered and faded by fatigue and trouble, how well the blow they had struck in the dark had taken effect.

Instead of taking the direct road down the high-street, Mme. Verdier followed the "garden path," as it was called, a long way round through the fields.

The birds sang to her as she passed, and the trees waved their white and perfumed flowers over her, as if nature were welcoming her with tender pity, seeking to restore to her in these short moments the gentleness and the love which the world had taken away. But the poor widow was unconscious of all this sweetness, for she was immersed in her grief.

When she got home she had to go to bed, for the fever had worn her out and her head was throbbing painfully.

.   .   .   .   .   .

Beneath the shade of an enormous oak, some forty students lay resting as they chatted together, some sitting, others stretched out at full length on the turf. Above them quivered thousands of leaves,

146

and the blue vault of heaven seemed to descend and to glide along the branches and through the foliage, mingling with all the greenery and filling it with sweetness, and tender, vaporous light.

The breeze passed gently over their heads and down into the plain, where it played on the golden waves of the harvest, making them sway gently as it passed.

The wind seemed like the soul of nature, vivifying, animating everything it touched, and bringing little quivers of new life to all things lulled by its caress.

The boys, too, felt the caress as it penetrated their senses, whispering in their hearts a longing for the holidays.

"Three more days," whispered the breeze; and in the depths of their being something answered:

"Three more days!"

Then, I know not how, the joy in their hearts broke forth in merry words and min-

147

gled laughter, until the birds in the trees above them became suddenly silent.

There was one boy, about fifteen years old, sitting at a distance from the rest, who formed no part of the merry group, and his sad face showed that he was not sharing in his comrades' happiness. It was Abel Verdier. Why was he sad? Had the dream he had abandoned returned to trouble his soul and fill it with regret? Why did he not rejoice too; he, the especial lover of Nature? She was so entrancing that evening, intoxicating the heart with her limpid murmurs and her fragrant sweetness!

Of what was he thinking?

Alas! It was not the past which troubled him, but the present, and especially the future. He was thinking of his mother, who at that moment was suffering for his sake—for his sake, whose dream had been one day to make her happy. And before his eyes spread no sweet vision like that which delighted his companions, but the vision of his mother's tears.

One of the group whispered in the ear of his companion, "See how troubled he looks now," and he nodded towards Abel.

"Yes," replied the other; "it is strange how he has changed of late; he who used to be so merry."

Yes, he had changed indeed, ever since he had received a letter from his mother in which she had told him what she was being made to suffer.

That evening, when they came in from their walk, Abel found a telegram from his mother telling him to come as quickly as possible, as she was ill. He left by the last train, three days before the holidays.

When he arrived home very late, he found his grandmother anxiously awaiting him.

His mother was in bed, but she was not asleep, and she was awaiting him also.

When he entered her room his heart stood still. He saw at a glance what she must have suffered. She, on her part, could not restrain her tears; and when they were quite alone she told him very gently all that she had not dared to write.

"You understand now," she said at length, "why I have sent for you. It was not for myself,—my illness is nothing,—but it was to tell you all that you must know. Forgive me for not having told you sooner; I was always waiting, hoping, up to the last moment, and I wanted to spare you pain."

Abel listened, and when his mother spoke of a distraint on her goods he grew rather pale and pensive, but seemed somewhat re-assured when he heard the amount of her debts. Then he consoled her, promising that he would have the seven hundred francs on the following day.

"Poor boy! From whom will you borrow? Nobody here dares any longer to do us any service!"

"Cheer up, little Mother; God has just given me an idea."

As Abel said these words, he placed his lips on her burning forehead, and she closed her eyes, reassured and almost happy.

CHAPTER VI

THE PRICE OF A VIOLIN

WHEN Abel was alone in his room, he took his violin from its case and gazed at it for a long time, and very sadly.

It was of this, his beloved violin, that he had thought when he had said to his mother:

"Cheer up, little Mother; God has just given me an idea."

He had thought of it in order to sell it, and to part from it for ever.

He remembered that his old master, M. Nirg, who was a lute-maker, had valued it at six hundred and fifty francs, and he resolved to take it to him on the following day. He decided to start very early in the morning, without saying anything to his mother. It was better that she should not know anything about it, for it would cause her too much sorrow.

He gazed at his beloved instrument as the light from the lamp shone on it, lighting up the varnish, and reflecting the graceful contour of the purfling on its sides. What a beautiful fiddle it was! How he loved it! It had belonged to his great-uncle, and then to his father, and it was in fact an heirloom, with many other memories attaching to it.

He remembered how, as a child, he had often begged his mother to open the case, promising not to touch it, so that he might see the violin lying there. It had no strings then, and he used to look at it pensively, knowing that something invisible and mysterious remained within it, which reminded him of his father, albeit the instrument was dead and sounded no more.

And then one day his mother had said

to him, "Take the violin; you are old enough now; it is yours," and he had pressed it joyfully in his arms, resting his childish head against it, and then he had felt the unknown something which he had divined trembling within the wood. And later on, when it had come to life again beneath his small, clumsy fingers, he and his mother had heard its voice, and the sound, as they recognized it, had brought tears to their eyes.

They wept because the voice, mysterious and far away as it sounded, and weak withal, as if time and distance had veiled it, was that which they had heard long years ago, and which now, after so long a silence, had suddenly awakened, issuing like a sigh from out the past, and reminding them of the loved one long vanished, who, as it were, had come to life again in the sound.

Since then, he had never been parted

154

from his fiddle, which had lulled his youth and sweetened the lives of those dear to him, the widow and her orphans, by restoring something of the joy of the past now removed by death.

His violin, like a dear friend, had been a partner in his life. He had made it the confidant of his thoughts, his hopes, and of his dreams,—of that too captivating dream which was destined never to be realized. And after his sacrifice, the violin was the only thing among his vanished illusions which remained to him, and it was the instrument which had laid his artistic regrets to rest, and which, up to yesterday, had helped him to forget his present anxieties.

And now he must sell it, and part from it for ever! He might not even blend his soul with its own in a last inspiration, in a final farewell, and thus engrave in his memory, for the last time, that voice, at once impressive and sad, which had sung to him through the years, chanting sometimes and weeping sometimes, and now to sound for him no more!

For the last time he pressed it to him and laid his lips against it. The violin gave forth a scarcely perceptible murmur as he touched it, as if something within it, connected with the past, had broken in answer to his farewell kiss.

Then Abel, with shining eyes, replaced the instrument in its long, coffin-like box, and knew that thenceforth it was dead to him.

Very early next day, after receiving from his grandmother the last news of the sick-room, Abel started, with his violin under his arm. He made a long detour through the fields so as to avoid seeing any one, and on arriving at the highroad he increased his pace, as if anxious to be free from his precious burden.

But while he walked on, he dared not think of what he was about to do.

Ere long he arrived at the little town of Milly. When he entered the workshop of his old master, he found him engaged in mending a cello. After giving him time to recover from his surprise at the unexpected meeting, Abel said to him pointblank:

"I want to sell my violin. You once valued it at six hundred and fifty francs. Should you be prepared to buy it at that price?"

"Of course I should! Why, I would give you seven hundred. But you are joking."

"No, I am not. I have given up studying the violin, and I want to get rid of my instrument."

"What a pity! Why, last year you were my best pupil."

"Last year!" repeated Abel, with a tender melancholy in his look and voice. "Many things have happened since last year."

The old violin-maker asked no further questions, but taking the violin from his former pupil, he pressed the strings, which, to Abel's fancy, groaned in reply, as if broken; then, pressing his large head heavily against the delicate and shining wood, he listened with his small, wrinkled ear as each sound died completely away.

Satisfied so far, he turned the instrument over in his hands, rapidly and minutely examining it; then, laying it on his worktable, he went off to find the money.

Abel, on receiving the notes, took one final look at his violin, that last memorial of his father, that great plaything which had fascinated his childhood and enchanted his youth, and which now belonged to him no more. Then he said good-bye to M. Nirg and departed.

As he passed the counter, with its violins, cellos and mandolins of all sizes and prices exposed for sale, he thought sadly:

"To-morrow my fiddle will be there too, and perhaps some rich passer-by, seeing that it is more beautiful than the others, will come in and buy it, and carry it far away, and I shall never know what has become of it. Ah, how the world can make one suffer, and how powerful is its hate!"

As he said these words to himself in a low voice, he left the town, following the white road which dips down into the valley with its ever changing and shimmering colours, while songs of birds, murmurs of insects and the scent of flowers greeted him as he passed. "Hatred! Why should it be?" he asked himself repeatedly, as his eye travelled over this kindly Nature, so full of love, who lavishes her riches on all, and scatters her graces and her innumerable charms in infinite condescension.

159

Yes; why should there be this hatred, when all around him so much love was lavished upon everything, making all live in a continual throbbing, and the songs of thousands of birds, and the perfumes of myriads of flowers, all wreathed in a sweet and tender harmony?

Why hate, when everything is made for love? For love makes the flower open her perfume to the murmuring bees, and love bends the reed which rocks the sleeping bird. And love brings the breeze to caress the shimmering leaves, making the birds to sing and the lark to mount to heaven and bathe herself in the light of the azure sky. And Mother Earth, too, who nourishes us, as she bares her breast to the ploughshare is content, for love constrains her.

Why then should there be hate?

Ah! Why this hate in man, and this love in Nature? Why should man deny and blaspheme God, while Nature ceaselessly

160

praises Him, sending up her voices in endless litanies and her perfumes in perpetual incense?

.   .   .   .   .   .

As Abel passed along, absorbed by these thoughts, a voice clear and pure issued from the branches close to him, and in spite of the sorrow at his heart he could not choose but listen.

He halted in gentle thoughtfulness, for he whom hatred was pursuing, and from whom it had taken his very means of song, would not disturb the little love-inspired songster, or cause that delicious voice to cease from its part in the world's oratorio.

All at once the sharp crack of a whip interrupted the small delicate voice, and immediately a fluttering of wings and a rustling of leaves were heard, and the bird flew off to resume her interrupted love-song farther away. Abel's eyes followed her lovingly.

"She at least," he thought, "can take refuge in the sky when the earth drives her away, and in the sky there is no hatred."

The boy continued on his way, and for a long time he walked without pausing. Before entering Vally he skirted the little wood which he had visited the day before he left for his apprenticeship, when he went for the last time to gaze on the objects he was about to quit. And then in that wood, so full of beauty, haunted by mysterious voices, he remembered that formerly he had so often dreamed of happiness, riches and honour, while what he had reaped was suffering, desertion and poverty.

.   .   .   .   .   .

The next day a bailiff well known in the neighbourhood, after spending a long time at the house of her principal enemy, entered Mme. Verdier's shop. His face wore an unaccustomed yet scarcely perceptible smile of content.

When he saw Abel coming towards him, he suddenly assumed a hard expression as if to impress the lad and to strike him with terror. He showed his brutality because he was sure that they could not pay what he was going to ask, and consequently they would be afraid of him.

Without replying to Abel's salutation, the man asked coldly for Mme. Verdier.

Abel explained that she was ill.

"Will you give her this paper?"

"That is not possible; she is asleep," said Abel firmly, inwardly delighted to be able to resist the man and to show that he did not fear him.

"It is a serious and important matter, and I can't come back."

"I know, Monsieur, that it is very serious," replied Abel ironically; "so I must ask you to be good enough to wait for a few minutes."

Young Verdier disappeared.

The man looked puzzled, wondering whether he was going to be paid.

Abel soon reappeared, holding in his hand seven blue sheets of paper, all that he had received in exchange for what was to him of inestimable value.

With what joy and triumph he unfolded and spread out the worn and faded notes required by the world, those notes which would prevent his enemies from satisfying their hate, but which had cost him so dear.

The bailiff, surprised, said nothing, but after rapidly verifying the notes, wrote out a receipt, folded them up, slipped them into his bag among several others, and took his departure.

Carry off those blue notes, thou blasé official, for they will prevent the poor grocer from being sold up, and show them to those who are waiting in the shadows for the accomplishment of the sinister work they have plotted; hasten, too, to those who sent thee, for doubtless they need the money—that money of the poor, whose real value thy employers will never know!

When his mother awoke, Abel showed her the receipt for the notes.

"Oh, thank you, thank you, my dear child! You have saved us! But how did you manage to get the money?"

"Later on I will tell you, Mother. Later on!"

The sick woman asked no more questions, and her sad eyes, which had so often wept, were lit by a serene joy.

She had been abandoned by all in her weakness, and now she felt the happiness of having a son at her side, and one who was bold and courageous, and who could defend her against her enemies.

Abel saw the joy in his mother's eyes, and forgetting what it had cost him, he rejoiced also, while down in the dark dwelling at the end of the village frustrated hate was redoubling its fury.

Abel rejoiced, but alas! not for long.

On the following day Mme. Verdier was worse, and the doctor, whom Abel pressed with questions, told him some dreadful things.

The sick woman was dying; her worn-out and anæmic body had no longer the force to recover, and unless she could have costly food and abundant nourishment, he could not hold out any hope.

Abel now realized that his mother was in serious danger, and that only unprocurable delicacies and the greatest care could restore her to health.

He understood, too, that no hope could be held out to a poor family which had not the means of purchasing the necessary things, and that while a rich woman might have been saved, for a poor one there was not the same chance.

When he comprehended the situation he suffered cruelly, but refusing to be discouraged, he wrote down the doctor's instructions and resolved to neglect nothing in order, if possible, to save his mother.

CHAPTER VII

FORGIVENESS

DURING the succeeding week there was an apparent improvement and Mme. Verdier seemed really better. Then the malady reasserted itself, and a further decline in strength took place.

Mme. Verdier's life was despaired of.

When the sad news spread through the village it produced a remarkable effect. People had not realized that she was so seriously ill, and at the thought that the "little grocer" was going to die they were horrified. Many among those who had left her and treated her with contempt, whether through hatred of religion, or through weakness of character, or because they were led away by others, now felt pity for the sick woman, and remorse at having made her suffer so cruelly.

Others, wishing to repair the mischief they had done, sent her all sorts of delicacies, tender bits of pigeon and chicken, eggs, cream and good old wine.

Mme. Verdier received these gifts joyfully.

"Do they then bear me no ill will?" she asked, now that they were proving themselves so charitable.

Alas! Charity which comes too late is useless. When she longed for these things, and when they might have saved her life, nothing was sent. Now, when all was of no use, she received gifts in abundance.

The poor sick woman could not help thinking of this; yet she was happy notwithstanding.

One day a rich woman, one who had been hard like so many others, came to see her

and asked her forgiveness, promising that
if the worst came to pass, she would be a
mother to little Joel and would receive the
old grandmother into her house.

Mme. Verdier accepted the offer with
tears in her eyes. She, the "little grocer,"
received plenty of visits now. All her old
customers came to see her, and to ask pardon
for having left her.

She saw nearly all of them: those who
had sent her away cruelly, others who had
simply declined her wares with an indifferent air, and those who had shamefacedly
asked her not to call again.

She knew they would come back, and
that they were not bad at heart, and she
forgot the past and refused to remember it.

And she received their stammering apolo-
gies with an indulgent smile which had a
gentle reproach in it, and which told clearly
enough that she had forgiven them.

And all these peasants, tender-hearted

at bottom, but who had been led away and made cruel by passion, party spirit and self-interest, now went away with sadness in their hearts,—those hearts which had once been so hard.

They went home, remembering what suffering they had caused to the poor little dealer, whom perhaps they would never see again in their village streets.

CHAPTER VIII

THE SECRET DISCLOSED

MME. VERDIER felt she was dying, and one day, when she saw the tears in Abel's swollen eyes, she made him sit down by her bedside and took his hand tenderly.

"My son," she began in a calm and caressing voice which made Abel sob, for he knew what she would say, "don't weep. I know I am going soon, and in a few more days I shall leave you. Don't weep, but be strong. You have faith, and you know that death is not the most terrible of trials. Ah! if you knew how sweet it is! If it were not for you, I should await it with joy, for I have suffered so much."

172

"For my sake," murmured Abel.

"No; you must not say that! It was not you, but the world and its hate. We have done our duty."

Abel no longer heard his mother. He was strangely pale. "Ah! Mother," he said, "if you knew what once——"

He could not go on; he was silent under the force of his emotion.

The sick woman saw that there was some secret which he wished to reveal, and she raised herself on her elbow and turned to him encouragingly.

"Speak, my boy, and tell me everything."

"Ah! little Mother, if you knew——"

And then, in a trembling voice which came straight from his heart, he told her the secret of his life, that which he had never revealed to a living soul.

He told her, as she lay broken and slowly dying from the torments and sufferings she had undergone, all about that dream, that beautiful dream of happiness which he had hoped to realize for her one day.

"If I have revealed this to you, little Mother,—this which I had resolved to keep for ever to myself,—it is in order that you may know, before you die, that I might have made you happy on earth; I might have worked on and become perhaps a brilliant artist."

"You will be a priest some day, 'Abel. I like better to think of you as that. You might have done as you say; you might have made me happy, but don't think of that, I shall have happiness above, and no one will be able to steal it from me. What am I saying? I have already experienced true happiness here, for, remember this, there is more happiness in strife and labour and sacrifice than in enjoyment and leisure. That is the Christian's happiness—to suffer well, and to die well. If you only knew

174

how happy I am to go! Especially after what you have just told me!

"No. I was not destined to know the happiness of this world, nor you either, poor child. You too must suffer as I have—nay, more than I. They will hate you, but do not envy them, for they will have less happiness than you will. Pity them, and in exchange for their hate give them love. Why do you weep?"

"Oh, if you could remain with me! If I could only hear your voice always!"

"It is true, my child, that you will be alone, and that I shall no longer be with you to defend and console you, and to remind you that hatred is nothing. I shall not be there to give you the love which the world will refuse you, but God will remain,— God, who never abandons His children and His apostles, and I shall pray so hard for you. And you, too—you will pray for me, little Abel?"

"O Mother!" sobbed the boy.

"You must say your first Mass for me. I had so longed to be present, and to see you go up to the altar. And I should have wished to hear you preach. You must often preach of death."

"Death!" repeated Abel, suddenly remembering that it was the thought of death which had brought him back to God. "Yes; I shall often preach of death."

There was a short silence. Each was thinking of what still remained to be said. Then the sick woman began to speak to him again, touching on the details of his future life and on his pastoral visits. When he returned in the evening he would not be alone, for she would be there and would speak to him.

O Mother tender and devoted! Mother stronger than death! She sought beforehand to live over the days when Abel would be left alone without her; she sought to speak now the words of affection which she would have spoken then, to soften the trials, to dry the tears which must flow, and to console his heart, which the world would surely wound.

She longed to give him now, at once, all the love and all the tenderness which she would have spread over his whole life, so as not to leave her place beside him quite a void.

She sought—not for herself, for death was sweet, but for the sake of her dear ones —to prolong the life which was ebbing away, and which they would miss so greatly.

During these last talks Abel would sit close to her, his eyes fixed on hers, gazing and listening as if to make up for the days when he would no longer be able to see her or to hear her.

Thus he made the most of his mother's last hours. Soon those mother eyes into whose depths he had so often lovingly gazed and wherein he had seen so many things, so many tears,—those eyes whose glance never left his face for a moment,—would look at him no more. The tender light which illumined them would be extinct.

And those lips which were now moving in prayer for him, which had given him so many kisses, so many tender and consoling words, would soon be motionless and dumb, with no further message for him. And all the intelligence, and the love and the memories of that dear face would have vanished.

These thoughts filled Abel's mind, and during those hours of sadness and discouragement he would often raise his eyes to the crucifix which hung above the sick-bed, where comfort is to be found, not only for those who are departing, but for those, too, who are left.

·   ·   ·   ·   ·   ·

One morning Mme. Verdier had a bad relapse, and Abel sent for the curé of

Eringes, who served the parish of Vally, to give her the last sacrament.

Towards evening her pain had gone, and she seemed better, but she had a presentiment of the approaching end.

"I feel that all is finished," she said to her son; "but before I go, tell me, as you promised, what you did to enable you to pay the draft. I must know all," she insisted as she saw him hesitate.

"What I did? Dearest Mother, if you *will* know, I sold my violin."

"Your violin! Your father's beautiful fiddle! Poor boy, what must it have cost you!"

The sick woman let her head fall back on the pillow, and her face, which had been so peaceful, grew troubled.

It was as if all that they had suffered, she and her son, and all the bitterness of sorrow which they had accumulated in their hearts, now reappeared manifestly in her poor wrinkled face so suddenly grown old.

Abel called his grandmother, who at once entered the room. When she saw her daughter, she, who had so often looked death in the face, understood at once. She came close to the bed.

"Yes, come, all of you," murmured Mme. Verdier. "Where is my little Joel? Is he still at school? How I wish I could take him in my arms once more! Take especial care of him."

The sick woman murmured a few words more, but they were too low to be audible. Her eyes seemed looking for something, and her long, thin hand wandered over the white sheets.

Abel took the crucifix from the wall and gave it to his mother. That was what she was looking for; her lifelong companion which had kept her kind-hearted in the midst of her enemies, which had shielded her in the past, and would support her in her last struggle.

As she pressed it fervently to her trembling lips, her drawn features grew calm, and the lines in her face seemed to disappear. The Figure on the cross smoothed away the traces of suffering, and left in their place, at the moment of death, an earnest of the eternal joy reserved for the departing soul.

Then the crucifix dropped with the hand which held it. She had departed with a smile.

Abel and his grandmother knelt long in the chamber of death, weeping and praying for her who could no longer see or hear them.

When little Joel returned that night from school, he was told that his mother had gone far, far away to a beautiful land; and the child understood that that land was called heaven,—the heaven which that night was coloured so deep and rich a blue.

CHAPTER IX

BY AN OPEN GRAVE

IT was a large crowd which followed the "little grocer" to her last resting-place, —so large that the churchyard was black with people.

It was a strange and astonishing phenomenon, this sudden change in a village which, now that it was too late, seemed bent on loving and lamenting her whom it had so long pursued with hatred. Nearly all the people who had watched the poor woman pass before their closed doors were now gathered at her tomb, and the remembrance of it all came back to them and filled their once hard eyes with tears.

It had taken a long time for compassion

to soften these men, hardened as they were by incredulity, egoism and self-interest; but now that pity had penetrated them, everything was changed. Pity had made them once more the sons of the peasants of olden days, with rough exteriors but soft hearts; true sons of those who loved because they believed.

Here and there a few words, interspersed with sobs, might be heard.

"How sad! We were all heartless. We may well weep for her now, for it's our fault that she is lying there."

And hands scarcely raised, and sorrowful gestures half concealed, pointed to the coffin at whose head knelt a young man and an old woman.

And these words which issued from the lips of a few of the spectators—mostly old men, for the old cannot contain what is in their hearts, as the young do—found an echo in the hearts of all. And all seemed to hear

183

the voices of their own departed ones reproaching them for this last death.

For this crowd, so agitated and so heartstricken, as it pressed around the bier, represented the repentance of a whole countryside. . . .

When the coffin was removed in order to lower it into the grave, a young man and an old woman came and stood on the brink.

They were Abel and his grandmother. Little Joel, too young for such scenes, had been left with the lady who had promised to be his foster-mother. The eyes of the young man and the old woman were filled with the same tears, and had in them the same farewell look.

The coffin remained for a moment suspended motionless over the grave; then the cords which held it were slowly paid out, and the coffin leaned suddenly to one side, and then gradually sank down and disappeared.

Abel gave vent to a cry of grief as he leaned forward to take a last look at the long, dark object which was vanishing with all that remained of her whom he had so greatly loved.

He bent long over that grave which had first taken his father from him, and now his mother also.

When he could see no more, he closed his eyes as if to recover his self-control; then, after looking at the earth which held the body, he gazed up to the heavens which held the soul. And in the midst of all his grief, he felt within him a great hope, as if his mother herself were supporting him, and here on the edge of the tomb of her who had sacrificed herself, he understood better what she had attempted, and comprehended as he had never done before the meaning of sacrifice, that great mainspring of human life, its beginning and its end.

And the words which his mother had

said to him when talking of happiness came back to him with a new comprehension:

"True happiness lies rather in self-sacrifice, in labour and in suffering, than in the selfish enjoyment and the leisure of a peaceful life."

By the open grave, above which Death hung poised like a bird of prey, he felt a new life rise within him, the true life which gives itself unstintedly, which offers itself in love, which is indispensable in sacrifice; and this life seemed to him to come from the land of the dead, from the earth where his ancestors reposed, where his mother too lay at rest.

And this new life changed and strengthened and transfigured him, increasing his courage and his faith in God.

Now that nothing held him back, he would give himself more completely to his work; he would shed abroad that life which he felt within him; he would continue to suffer and to love.

Abel, and his grandmother after him, took up the brush and dropped the holy water over the grave in the sign of the cross. Then they turned and went out of the churchyard, through the ranks of the weeping crowd.

CHAPTER X

THE KILLING OF HATE

THAT evening, after the funeral, six persons—the same whom we have more than once met—assembled in the mysterious dwelling.

Who were these men who had slowly murdered the poor dealer? Who were they? What was their sect? Reader, you know!

On their sinister faces could be read dismay and disappointment, and at the back of their evil-looking eyes, which had just gazed on the corpse of their unhappy victim, could be seen an expression of baffled anger.

Yet their enemy was dead!

Aye, she was dead, but the whole country-side was weeping for her!

Yes, she was dead, that poor widow, that humble dealer so retiring and so gentle, that brave, strong mother who had refused to withdraw her son from the seminary, or to take back her gift to God. She was dead, and yet these powerful and dangerous men, these enemies to the faith, who had gained a whole parish to their side, who had made two children orphans,—these men felt that they had been vanquished.

They realized that all the hate they had sown in the hearts of their neighbours after months and months of labour, had been broken down by the faith and love of one weak woman.

O Faith, that makest love stronger than hate,—ancient and much-loved Faith of my country,—never shalt thou be torn from its beloved soil!

Still shalt thou thrill the hearts of her

189

children; nor shall the unbeliever, in his hate, prevail to drive thee from this land of ours, where the ashes of our dead call thee, and the blood of our martyrs holds thee fast!

Here shalt thou abide so long as sons of France, however poor, however bereft, owning perhaps nought but a dream, shall give up their all to become thy defenders!

No! most precious, most tender Faith, taught us at our mother's knee, never shalt thou die out in our dear country, so long as Christian mothers, even the poorest, are content to suffer for thee, and to give to God, despite the hatred of the world, their true riches and their chief hope—the children of their love!